Napoleon Hill's PMA: Science of Success -

An Introduction

by Dr. Robert C. Worstell,

based on notes from Napoleon Hill's lectures

Table of Contents

To all our many devoted and loyal fans:

We produce these editions <u>only</u> for you.

(Be sure to get your bonuses at the end of the story...)

- - - -

Look for addtional versions of this book in print, audio, and course formats. Ask your bookseller for the versions you want - see also the Related Books section at the end.

Editor's note: In early 1954, Napoleon Hill and W. Clement Stone created a short series of thirteen TV shows that promoted what was later finalized into Hill's PMA: Science of Success Course. Through these short episodes, Hill explained in simple terms what was to become the final polished version of his Personal Philosophy of Success, and a final update to Hill's perennial bestselling "Think and Grow Rich".

The chapters below are derived from my own notes of those lectures. These chapters have been edited and arranged in sequence for the simple learning and application. This book is written to emulate Napoleon Hill's lecture style, in modernized language. So you can consider that Hill is talking to you directly through these pages.

My own work in this book is to enable his televised talks to become more accessible to you and everyone. This book is for your *immediate* use in improving your own life and achieving everything you want out of life.

At the end of this book, you'll find a complete listing of the PMA: Science of Success lessons and where to apply to start your own self-paced course, starting now.

past or present publishers of Napoleon Hill's various books and other materials.

Introduction

DURING HIS LIFETIME of research, Napoleon Hill studied success. And became a millionaire three times over as a result. One of his students, W. Clement Stone, persuaded him to come out of retirement and polish his practical approach to a final course. To those two we owe an intense debt. For without their persistence, we would not have this goldmine at our fingertips today.

Hill made several approaches to this philosophy, each of which wound up as published bestsellers in their day. He's most known for his "Think and Grow Rich" which is still anecdotally known as the one book that has made more millionaires than any other single published work.

In his final version, which he promoted in various lectures, Hill condensed his wealth of material into 17 principles. These were distilled from a lifetime of study to discover, test and promulgate the common successful principles that the successful used consistently to create their success.

As such, they are natural principles and not subject to the whims of technological advances or marketing fads and gimmicks. They have existed through the long written and verbal histories and philosophies of humankind in different formats and descriptions. Hill's life-work has been to distill them into a simple, workable course of study and promote that system broadly.

What you have in your hand is a small handbook that introduces you to his final distilled principles.

In the back, you'll see where additional books, courses and materials enlarge on these 17 principles. And as you study this book, you'll see more and more of these principles start to show up in other works you study. Because they are principles of Nature. Our job is to observe them for ourselves, test them fully with our own applications, and then help others to have their own success through their own observation and self-tests.

This study is a life-journey you are embarking on.

You'll find in your studies that the principles are interlocked with each other. This is because they are a complete system. Each of the principles influence the others. And their composite whole produces a much greater result than the effect of each individual principle applied separately. And so it's recommended you study this book several times over and look for new applications and interactions each time. Practice these principles in your life, test them each individually for yourself as well testing them as a whole system.

You'll see that the greater good you help others to achieve will bring you the assistance you need for your own success. The greater help you give, the greater value you provide to others around you, the greater returns will come your way.

It all starts with your choosing a definite purpose and aligning your life actions to achieving, acquiring, or attaining that purpose.

There are no limits except those you've accepted for yourself. Truly, "whatever you can conceive and believe, you can achieve."

So, take our best wishes with you on your own journey to all the happiness, joy, and success that is possible through these natural principles.

Begin today. The second best time to start is Now.

Dr. Robert C. Worstell, October 2020

Your Mindset

"A Positive Mental Attitude is the right mental attitude for each given set of circumstances. It is most often comprised of the plus characteristics symbolized by such words as faith, integrity, hope, optimism, courage, initiative, generosity, tolerance, tact, kindliness and good common sense."

From "Success Through A Positive Mental Attitude", by Napoleon Hill and W. Clement Stone.

Whatever You

Can CONCEIVE and BELIEVE,

You Can ACHIEVE!

HOW TO STUDY THIS COURSE

═══

THE PMA PHILOSOPHY STIMULATES THE MIND AND CAUSES THE BIRTH OF SCORES OF IDEAS!

Napoleon Hill taught many hundreds of thousands of people – who read his books, studied his PMA SCIENCE OF SUCCESS COURSE, and/or attended his lectures — the true meaning of this premise. By studying this Course as it is meant to be studied, you too will DEVELOP SUCCESS HABITS. It is urged that:

As you study this course, study it for a purpose.

• Continually SEARCH the course for ways to achieve your goals and/or how to solve your problems.

• CONCENTRATE as you study. Study as though Napoleon Hill has personally written to you — and you alone.

• KNOW WHAT YOU ARE LOOKING FOR. Commit yourself to Recognizing, Relating, Assimilating and Applying the principles, techniques and ideas that this course provides to you.

─────────

IDEAS COME FROM UNEXPECTED PLACES! It is therefore important that you study with a pen or pencil in hand — ready to underscore or jot down in the margins of your lesson-book, anything of interest; a flash of inspiration or an answer to your problem. This principle also applies to any other books or articles you may read, lectures you attend, or from watching films or television.

The universal principles contained in your PMA Science of Success Course are designed to stimulate the imaginative facilities of your brain and nervous system so that they will create new and usable ideas for you. As you study, ask yourself, "WHAT DOES THIS MEAN TO ME AND HOW CAN I USE IT?"

You should be alert for each "HOW TO" as well as its component, "WHAT TO DO," as there is a direct relationship between the two. The answers are there!

Develop good study habits. Set aside a specific time each day to study your lessons. We recommend studying approximately 15 minutes a day. Make certain that it is a time that your mind is most alert and receptive to new ideas. Discipline yourself to STUDY EVERY DAY — never allowing yourself to skip days.

Choose a location to study where you will be comfortable and unlikely to be disturbed. Try using the same place every day.

When starting each new lesson, we recommend that you read it through from start to finish — stopping only to mark what you feel is important; what you would like to memorize. Or, put a question mark by the statements that you don't quite understand. This is also an excellent time to jot down any inspiring ideas or potential solutions to problems that you might have. Try hard to complete the lesson before you stop reading.

Always keep in mind your Definite Action Plan, read and study your lesson once again; making certain that you comprehend the information in each paragraph. Look up all words that you do not understand in your dictionary being certain to note its SYNONYMS. Tab and dog-ear pages, highlight, and/or underline every phrase and sentence of importance to you. Feel free to keep notes separately as you go.

You will find it helpful to then reread each lesson a third time. That reading, and all subsequent ones, will help reinforce what you have already learned and perhaps help you memorize self-motivators that now appeal to you.

The way of success is the way of *action*, based upon organized thinking followed by action, action, action.

To fully achieve the goals of your life, STUDY . . . THINK . . . PLAN . . . and APPLY the PRINCIPLES that this course will provide for you. Once you have SUCCESSFULLY completed the 17 lessons contained in the full PMA SCIENCE OF SUCCESS COURSE, you will find that your subconscious mind always reacts positively for you. THEN AND ONLY THEN WILL YOUR DOOR TO SUCCESS BE OPEN TO YOU.

I – Goal Achievement

Definite Purpose

DEFINITENESS OF PURPOSE is the first and most basic step and the first clue to the system of individual achievement which itself underlies all great successes in every calling in every part of the world.

Psychologists have discovered a natural law which is the very foundation of all personal successes, and I can describe it to you in one short sentence so you can understand it:

Whatever the mind can conceive and believe the mind can achieve.

You will notice that it says nothing about the need for structured schooling and academic degrees, but simply that whatever your mind can conceive and believe your mind can achieve. Now, if you want evidence that such can be accomplished without the benefit of formal education, you all have to remember that Thomas A. Edison conceived the idea of becoming an inventor and lived to become the world's greatest scientist in the field of invention with only *three months* of common school education.

I was first challenged by Andrew Carnegie to research and document this set of natural principles – those that make it possible for you and I and everyone else to write his own price tag in life and attain it. That research and documentation took the rest of my life to this point where I delivered these lectures. That research was paid for without any grant or outside financing, but through use of the Science of Success Philosophy itself – just as it was discovered, tested, and refined. You have in your hands today what is close to a final summation of over 50 years of study and testing.

My search led me to study the spiritual forces that we are all blessed with. And it was in this field that I came upon a clue which has enabled me to help millions of people to find success in their earthly destinies.

I want to describe my discovery in the simplest terms possible. And so reveal to you just how that one statement above is true, regardless of how many times you may have failed in the past – or how any your most lofty aims and hopes may seem out of reach right now.

———————

I FIRST GOT A FLEETING glimpse of the profound principle of the Definite Purpose while I was being coached by Andrew Carnegie.

I had just finished telling Mr. Carnegie that I feared he had chosen the wrong person to give the world the first practical philosophy of personal success – because of my youth, my lack of education, and my lack of finances. Well, at this point, Mr. Carnegie delivered a lecture that I will never forget because it changed my entire life. And that talk paved the way for my helping to change the lives of millions of people, some of them not yet born.

"Let me call your attention to a great power which is under your control," said Mr. Carnegie. "A power which is greater than poverty, greater than the lack of education, greater than all of your fears and superstitions combined.

"It is the power to take possession of your own mind and direct it to whatever ends you may desire.

"This profound power," Mr. Carnegie continued, "is the gift of the Creator. And it must have been considered the greatest of all of his gifts to man – because it is the only thing over which man has the complete and unchallengeable right of control and direction.

"When you speak of your poverty and lack of education," Mr. Carnegie explained, "you are simply directing your mind power to attract these undesirable circumstances. Because it is true that whatever your mind feeds upon, your mind attracts to you. Now you see why it is important that you recognize that all success begins with definiteness of purpose – with a clear picture in your mind of precisely what you want from life."

Then Mr. Carnegie continued his speech with a description of a great universal truth. This made such an impact upon my mind that I began then and there to give myself a new outlook on life. As a result, I set up for myself a goal so far above my previous achievements that it shocked my friends and relatives when they heard about it.

"Everyone," said Mr. Carnegie, "comes to the earth plane blessed with the privilege of controlling his mind power and directing it to whatever ends he may choose. But everyone also brings over with him at birth the equivalent of two sealed envelopes.

"One of which is clearly labeled 'the **riches** you may enjoy if you take possession of your own mind and direct it to ends of your own choice.'

"And the other is labeled 'the **penalties** you must pay if you neglect to take possession of your mind and direct it.'"

"And now let me reveal to you," said Mr. Carnegie, "the contents of those two sealed envelopes. "In the one labeled '**riches**' is this list of blessings.

"*One*: sound health.

"*Two*: peace of mind.

"*Three*: a labor of love of your own choice.

"*Four*: freedom from fear and worry.

"*Five*: a positive mental attitude.

"*Six*: material riches of your own choice and quantity.

"In the sealed envelope labeled '**penalties**,'" Mr. Carnegie continued, "Is this list of the prices one must pay for neglecting to take possession of his own mind.

"*One*: ill health.

"*Two*: fear and worry.

"*Three*: indecision and doubt.

"*Four*: frustration and a discouragement throughout life.

"*Five*: poverty and want.

"*Six*: and a whole flock of evils consisting of envy, greed, jealousy, anger, hatred, and superstition."

NOW, MY MISSION IN life has from that point forward to help you, and everyone who needs my help, to open up and use the contents of the sealed envelope labeled "riches." This is the starting point from which you must take off. If you wish to write your own ticket from here on out for the remainder of your life, I will describe these simple instructions for you:

One: procure a neat, pocket-sized notebook. And on page one *write down a clear description of your major desire in life*. Write out the one circumstance or position or thing which you will be willing to accept as your idea of success. And remember, before you begin writing, that your only limitations are those which you set up in your own mind or permit others to set up for you.

Two: on page two of your notebook, *write down a clear statement of precisely what you intend to give in return* for that which you desire from life. And then start in, right where you stand now, to begin giving.

Three: *memorize both of your statements*; what you desire and what intend to give in return for it – and then repeat them both at least a dozen times daily.

Always end your statements with a expression of gratitude for the blessings with which you were gifted at birth, such as:

> *"I ask not for divine providence, for more riches, but more wisdom with which to accept and use wisely the riches I received at birth in the form of the power to control and direct my mind to whatever ends I desire."*

If you are not already too successful or self-satisfied to accept and express such a profound prayer, and if you accept it and express it in the same spirit of humble sincerity in which I pass it on to you – a new and a better world will reveal itself to you, a world in which you will see reflected the circumstances and the things which you yourself have created.

Master Mind

WE COME NOW TO THE second principle which leads to the attainment of your definite major purpose in life.

This principle of success is called the **mastermind principle**.

An understandable definition of the mastermind is this:

> *A mastermind consists of two or more people who work in perfect harmony for the attainment of a definite purpose.*

Now here are some interesting facts about the mastermind which give you an idea of how important it is – and how necessary that you embrace this principle and make use of it in attaining success in your chosen occupation.

First of all, it is the principle through which you may borrow and use the education, the experience, the influence, and perhaps the capital of other people in carrying out your own plans in life. It is the principle through which you can accomplish more in one year than you could accomplish without it in a lifetime – if you depended only on your own efforts for success.

This one is one fact that I am absolutely certain: *when you form a true mastermind alliance with others and work with them in a spirit of perfect harmony, you can draw freely upon the spiritual forces within you for carrying out your plans and desires.*

I also know that the mastermind principle can give you absolute protection against failure, provided always that your purpose in using this principle is beneficial to all you influence.

IN MY RESEARCH, WHILE organizing the science of success, I had the collaboration of practically every outstanding successful man this country has produced during the past 50 years – and I can tell you definitely that their success was due in the main to their knowledge and application of this mastermind principle.

I also want to call your attention to the fact that our great American way of life – and our unmatchable system of free enterprise – have been built upon this mastermind principle. The greatest document ever conceived by the mind of man is a perfect example of the mastermind principle in action. It is the Declaration of Independence. And the best evidence of the importance of maintaining perfect harmony in a mastermind alliance may be found in the fact that the fifty-six men who signed the Declaration of Independence knew full well that it might turn out to be either a license of freedom for all mankind, or a death warrant that would cause each of the signers to be hanged.

NOW LET US SEE HOW the mastermind principle has brought success to people whom we all know.

First consider when Kate Smith began her career as a singer. She had difficulty in earning enough from her singing to pay her living expenses and she perhaps never would have made her singing pay if she had not discovered and applied the mastermind principle when she formed the mastermind alliance with Ted Collins. And according to a report I saw in "Reader's Digest," Kate Smith had already earned upwards of $30 million and she was still in the upper brackets of income for her profession at that time.

I remember when Edgar Bergen and that cute little block of wood known as Charlie McCarthy used to play anywhere they could get an engagement. And I rather suspect that often all they got for their services was a meal. But Edgar Bergen was a smart man in the field of entertainment. So he formed a mastermind alliance which introduced him and Charlie to millions of people by radio and television. Bergen was never short of income or performances for the rest of his life.

You may be surprised when I tell you that the great Ford industrial empire started with the formation of a mastermind alliance between Henry Ford and his wife. At the beginning of his career, Henry Ford was shy and lacking in self-confidence. It was Mrs. Ford who inspired Henry Ford with the faith and the courage to go ahead with the perfection of his horseless carriage. Even though his relatives and neighbors generally tried to discourage him from wasting his time with the "contraption", as they called it.

The federation of states known as the United States of America is the richest and the most powerful nation civilization has yet produced. And the secret of our strength and riches consists in our form of government – where all our states function in a spirit of harmony, based on the mastermind principle, through a central federal government located at Washington.

AND NOW A WORD TO YOU personally. If you work for a salary or wages, you have a marvelous opportunity to promote yourself into a higher income and a more responsible position by forming a mastermind alliance with your associate workers, including the management.

I'll give you further instructions in the next chapter on how to apply the mastermind principle so as to increase your own income and promote yourself to a higher position with the full cooperation of your management. I'll show you how to write your own price tag, fix your own wages, establish your own working hours, and give yourself financial independence. Before that chapter, you need to do three things to get the most benefit of what I'm about to tell you.

> **First**, decide definitely where you wish to be and what you wish to be doing during the next three years.

> And **second**, decide how much money you desire to be making and what you are going to do to earn it.

> And **third**, form a mastermind alliance with at least one person in your immediate family and at least one other person among those to whom you are selling your services.

By taking these three steps, you will have gone a long way toward appropriating the great master key to success.

There is no such thing as getting something for nothing. Everything, including your personal success, has a price that must be paid. And the only price necessary to pay right now is to do the three simple things that I just suggested.

Now, before you begin to take action on the three steps, there is one important fact I wish to you to remember and it is this:

> *Control your mental attitude and make yourself friendly and agreeable with everyone who you are closely associated – if you expect friendly cooperation in return.*

Indifference cannot create a mastermind alliance for you.

A negative mental attitude can bring you nothing but failure.

Remember always, you are *where* you are and *what* you are because of the mental attitude you have when when you relate to other people.

Remember also, your mental attitude is the one and the only thing over which you have complete control.

SUCCESS IS SOMETHING which has to be planned and success is something which has to be earned in advance. Again, you have to give before you can get. True, there is such a thing as luck, but just remember that luck is something you can create for yourself if you know the rules and follow them just as I give them to you.

Remember too that success in the higher brackets of achievement is something that can be had only by taking others along with you. And the best definition of success which I know is this:

> *Success is the progressive realization of a worthy goal – without violating the rights of others, and by helping others to acquire it.*

There is a known formula for the attainment of success and it is just as definite and certain as are the rules of mathematics or the rigorous analysis of science.

My purpose in these chapters is to bring you that formula in simple terms that you can understand and apply. But I can only give you something you are ready for it. If you are ready to advance into the higher brackets of success, you will recognize this fact by your willingness to follow the simple instructions I'll give you as we go along.

If Kate Smith had not been ready for success when she formed the mastermind alliance with Ted Collins, he couldn't have brought her success. This thing called success is a very profound and interesting thing because the line of demarcation between success and failure is so slight that it is often hard to tell where one ends and the other begins.

For example, in my association with the late Henry Ford, I recognize that he had thousands of people working for him who had much more education than he, more magnetic personalities, more ability to make friends, and a much better chance of succeeding than Mr. Ford had when he was working for wages, but Mr. Ford had one simple quality the others who worked for him did not possess, which made him the greatest industrialist this nation has ever produced.

In the next chapter, I'll give you a definite clue as to the success quality which helped Henry Ford spread his influence throughout the world and to make himself quite rich, despite the fact that he had only a meager common school education.

Until then, please realize that your only real limitation is the one you accept and set up in your own mind.

Applied Faith: Persistence

LET'S INTRODUCE YOU to your greatest asset.

The name of this principle is **applied faith**, and I want you to remember it.

It is not something I am bringing to you, but it is something you already possess, although you may not have used it much before now.

> *Applied faith is the mental attitude that clears your mind of all fears and doubts and direct your mind to the attainment of whatever you desire in life.*

Persistence is just another word for applied faith. The difference between persistence and lack of it is the same as the difference between wishing for a thing and positively determining to get it.

In the first chapter, I told you that you and I and every person were blessed with the privilege of complete control over but one thing – and that is the exclusive right to take possession of our own minds and direct them to the attainment of whatever we desire in life.

Applied faith is a mental attitude we must cultivate and maintain before we can take complete possession of our minds. It is the means by which we may break the seal of that "riches" envelope I mentioned earlier. You take full possession of the six forms of riches when you consciously take possession of your own conceiving and believing.

Those six riches were, as you may remember, sound health, peace of mind, a labor of love of your own choice, freedom from fear and worry, a positive mental attitude, and material riches of your own choice and quantity.

IN ORDER THAT YOU MAY condition your mind to embrace and use applied faith, you must understand that there are two ways in which you can use faith. You can put it into reverse gear and use it in a negative way by allowing your mind to dwell upon the circumstances and the things you do not want, such as poverty, ill health, failure, defeat, and this is precisely what the majority of people do, which explains why the majority of people go through life in misery and want.

Or you can take possession of your mind and direct it to think of the six riches which came over with you in that sealed envelope, and you will attract these riches to bless and serve you all through the rest of your life.

Now, let me give you a description of the one thing which represents the main difference between a successful person and a failure. Please pay attention, and think for yourself as you read these words. Because failure to recognize the truth I am about to give you is the starting point of most failures.

Successful people, in all occupations, all profession, and all callings, have one trait which distinguishes them from the failures: It is their capacity for belief.

The failures see the hole in the donut but do not see the donut around the hole. The successes see the hole also, but they focus on the donut around the hole.

Thomas A. Edison believed that he could perfect an incandescent electric lamp, and despite the fact that he failed over 10,000 times before he was crowned with success, he made his belief uncover the secret for which he was searching. Give one guess as to how many times the average person must fail before he quits, fails because of the lack of capacity for belief. How many times can you meet with defeat before you give up the ghost and quit?

Henry Ford believed he could build a self-propelled vehicle which would take the place of the horse and buggy, and despite the ridicule of relatives and neighbors and the lack of finances, he transmuted his belief into an industrial empire which changed the entire American way of life. Mind you, Ford did this with very little education and no operating capital to begin with.

Right here, let me ask you a question which may well change your entire life. You, perhaps, have an idea or a plan which would be useful to other people, but you have done nothing about it because you lack the self-confidence to give you a start. In other words, you're now where Henry Ford was before he built the first model of his world-famous automobile. Mr. Ford broke through that wall of fear, which may now be holding you back, and put his idea into operation by making use of the mastermind principle I mentioned in our second chapter — through an alliance with his wife.

Now, the question I wish to ask you is this: why don't you form a mastermind alliance with someone and begin putting your ideas to work for you? "Belief" is truly a magic word because it is the beginning of all successes. It is the very foundation of civilization. It is the one quality you must develop before you can make use of the great master key to success.

TO BE SUCCESSFUL, YOU must become a person with a great capacity for belief, and the place to start believing is with yourself. Begin by recognizing that you were born with the opportunity for complete personal control over your own mind.

Also recognize that by the application the material in this book, you can take full possession of your mind and make it yield you whatever you demand in life.

Observe I use the word "demand," not "beg." The Creator never intended for you to *beg* for anything. If he had, he would not have blessed you with full control over your own mind.

If your life is not what you want it to be, you can change it. As a matter of fact, you can do anything, within reason, that you desire to do – *if* you embrace the principle of applied faith and keep it directed to the attainment of the things you want and off the things you do not want.

I should know what I'm talking about because I was handicapped at birth by the Four Horsemen which keep most people in bondage all the days of their lives: poverty, fear, illiteracy, and superstition. In theory, I didn't have the slightest reason to hope that I could ever escape the influences of these four curses, but I did escape, and now I am devoting my entire life to helping other people to gain deliverance from these four basic enemies of mankind.

———————————

I GIVE YOU NOW THESE instructions that you can use to create a mental attitude favorable for expressing faith.

One, *know* what you want and *believe* that you can and will get it.

Two, give expressions of gratitude many times daily for having received that which you want, even before you actually get physical possession of it. Possession starts first in the mind. Please remember this.

Third, keep your mind open for hunches from within, and when you are inspired to action, do not wait, but move on your own personal initiative at once. Remember, there can be no application of applied faith without action.

Fourth, when overtaken by defeat, as you may be many times, remember that man's faith is tested many times before he is crowned with final victory. Accept your defeat as nothing more than a challenge to keep on trying.

Five, developing a burning desire for the things or circumstances you want. That is the starting point of all applied faith. Be definite. Believe and act. And keep on acting, if at first you meet with defeat.

Six, when doubt creeps into your mind, remember that "...whatsoever a man believeth, that will he also reap".

- Also remember that faith is not something you *get*. Faith is something you *already have*, but you may be using it in reverse gear by believing in the circumstances and things you do not want, the things you fear.

- And remember that faith is *guidance only*. It is not a power which will bring you what you want but a power that can guide you to go after what you want and get it.

- Remember, too, that your faith is limited only by your own capacity to *believe*. You can do whatever you make up your mind to do.

I believed I could give the world a practical philosophy of success which would free men and women from their fears and limitations. I stood firmly back of that belief through 50-odd years of effort, and I've seen my beliefs give freedom to millions of people.

"Do the thing," said Emerson, "and you will have the power."

Another phrase for this is "believe and you will receive".

Also remember that your life is *exactly* what you make it by your own mental attitude.

II - Accurate Focus

Self Discipline

THIS CHAPTER BRINGS us to the eighth principle of success. Without this one principle, the preceding principles I have given you previously would be useless.

It is the principle of self-discipline.

Self-discipline, as I am presenting it to you here, refers not only to your mastery of negative habits which keep you from your success – but more particularly to develop and enforce positive habits you will need, to fully utilize those six life-assets from that sealed envelope I mentioned in the first chapter.

Now here's a list of the more important things which you will have to use your self-discipline to control before you can fully internalize and use this system of 17 principles fully.

One: you will have to gain mastery over your tongue by acquiring the habit of thinking first and then speaking – after you are sure that what you say will benefit you and not injure others. A loose tongue often is one's greatest liability.

Two: you will have to exercise self-discipline in mastering the common tendency to strike back at those who you feel a cause, real or imaginary, for a grievance. You must remember that everything you do to or for another, you do to or for yourself, because your every thought and every act which benefits or injures another person comes back to you in kind, greatly multiplied. If you feel that you must slander another person, do not speak it, but write it. Write it in the sands near the water's edge, then move away from it until the tides have flown.

Three: you will have to exercise self-discipline over all of your emotions, particularly your emotions of love, hate, fear, and sex. These are the big four of your emotions, and they can make you or break you, according to the extent of discipline you exercise over them.

Four: your mental attitude needs discipline and control at all times. Lacking this discipline, it can and it often does drive away friends, destroy opportunities to get ahead, brings on physical and mental illness, develops stomach ulcers and... makes peace of mind impossible.

Five: I have reserved the emotion of sex for special mention, because failure to exercise self-discipline over this emotion probably heads the list of all the causes of personal failure. The emotion of sex is the most powerful of all emotions, and it is nature's great creative instrument with which all species of living things are perpetuated. The proper means of using self-discipline over the emotion of sex is transmutation – the control and direction of this great emotional feeling toward the attainment of worthy purposes – such as the fulfillment of one's major purpose in life.

The great leaders, artists, orators, industrialists, and professional people have learned the art of sex transmutation through the proper system of self-discipline. Because of the delicacy of the subject of sex emotion, I am limited as to the information I can give you about it in this chapter. But I have covered the subject much more in detail in some of my books.

And **six:** your stomach also needs discipline through the proper habits of dieting and fasting. Because information on dieting and fasting should come from your own doctor, I will not go into details concerning them except to call your attention to the need for knowledge on this subject.

And **seven:** you will need to exercise self-discipline in relation to religion and politics. Because our country, which is the most acceptable form of society civilization has yet produced, is made up of people of varying beliefs in connection with both of these subjects. To be happy and prosperous in our country, we must learn to live and to let live, to give others the privileges we ask and demand for ourselves – and this often calls for strict discipline over self.

Eight. But I have reserved until the last my reference to the most important circumstances over which you must exercise the strictest of self-discipline if you are to embrace and use these course principles. I refer to your profound privilege of taking possession of your own mind and directing it to whatever ends you may desire.

You cannot take possession of your own mind or direct it to definite ends without a practical system. I have devoted the better portion of my past life to the revelation and presentation of such a system, and I know that this system works because it has been successfully used by many millions of people throughout the world.

The system is not only practical and workable, but it is so simple that anyone who is ready for it may master it and use it successfully.

Its use does not call for a genius nor a great amount of formal education. It calls only for a will to take possession of one's own mind and a definite purpose to which the mind is to be directed.

The self-discipline used by Thomas A. Edison made him the world's greatest inventor – who revealed to mankind during the first half of the 20th century more of nature's secrets than had been uncovered during the entire previous history of civilization.

Self-discipline carried Wilbur and Orville Wright through a multitude of failures and enabled them finally to give the world its first practical airplane. And their achievement has made the world smaller and changed the entire trend of civilization.

Self-discipline helped Helen Keller to triumph over deafness, blindness, and dumbness – a combination of afflictions such as most people never experience.

Self-discipline helped me to carry on, through years of heart-aching discouragement and defeat, to give the world the first practical philosophy of success based on the combined know-how gained by studying the successes of hundreds of men and women. Each of them in turn had spent a lifetime on their own, by the trial-and-error method, in discovery of these principles which lead to their personal success.

Self-discipline is among the top-ranking features of all the great religions, including Christian, Buddhist, Taoist, and other faiths.

And there are some people who believe that our major purpose on Earth is that of developing wisdom through struggle and self-discipline.

One thing is certain. No one ever becomes very wise without the aid of self-discipline, and no one ever finds peace of mind and happiness without the strict exercise of self-discipline.

Self-discipline is the only means of transmuting sorrow into faith. It is the only means by which we may transmute hatred of others into the milder emotion of sympathy for them.

It is the only means by which we may reveal and profit by the seed of an equivalent benefit which comes with every adversity and every defeat.

It is the only means by which we may shut out of our minds the deadly effects of past experiences of suffering and unpleasantness.

And it is the means by which we may discover that other self we carry around with us, that self which has great capacity for belief and does not become influenced by failure and defeat.

Self-discipline can give us freedom from the fear of death, the most difficult to master of all of our fears. It can free us from the disease of hypochondria, the fear of imaginary illness, with which so many people suffer and sometimes die.

Self-discipline is the means by which we may think our own thoughts, live our own lives as we wish to live them, and remain forever free from the evils of fears and limitations – which we have inherited from the dark ages before the dawn of civilization.

The Creator never gives one an asset or benefit without passing along also the means of how it can be embraced and used. Self-discipline, therefore, is the means by which the Creator provided us with a method of embracing and using the only thing over which we have unchallengeable control: *the power of our own thoughts.*

Accurate Thinking

THE RULES OF ACCURATE thinking are so clear and simple that I often wonder why so few people ever take time to learn the rules. Accurate thinking is the very foundation of all successful achievements.

Here's a working description of the rules of accurate thinking, which all successful people follow:

First of all, *accurate thinking is based on two simple fundamentals.* They are called inductive reasoning and deductive reasoning.

Inductive reasoning is used when the necessary facts on which to base your thinking are not available. In this case, you act on hypotheses or what you assume the facts to be.

Deductive reasoning is used when you have the facts or what appear to be the facts on which to base your thinking.

The **next** step in accurate thinking is to *separate facts from fiction or hearsay evidence* and determine whether you are dealing with hypotheses or real facts.

When you are sure you base your thinking on dependable facts, you take the second step by separating these facts into two classes. One is the important facts, and the other is unimportant facts.

When you do this, you may be surprised at the overwhelmingly greater number of unimportant facts you deal with daily than important facts.

How can you distinguish an important from an unimportant fact? An important fact is *any fact that will aid you to any extent at all in attaining the object of your major purpose in life.*

And *all* other facts, as far as you are concerned, are <u>unimportant</u>, and you should waste no time with them.

You can employ reading this chapter to great benefit if you will do this:

Take a moment to write out a list on paper of all the facts you dealt with yesterday, separating them into two classes – important and unimportant. Actually, you will make a big discovery regarding accurate thinking if you adopt this as a habit. At the same time each day, make a list of all the facts that got your attention that day, placing them in two separate columns – one labeled "important facts" and the other labeled "unimportant facts." Look them over and make your own conclusions.

Now let's take up the subject of *opinions* – and see what loose, unsound opinions are mistaken for accurate thinking.

To start with, the truth is that most opinions are without value because they are based on bias, prejudice, intolerance, guesswork, hearsay evidence, and out-and-out ignorance.

These may seem harsh words I'm using, but they represent most of the sources life's tragedies that people run into unnecessarily.

And of the tragedies which cause misery and failure, none are more merciless or destructive than those that grow out of a person's indifference to learning how to think accurately.

I will never forget an experience I had with President Woodrow Wilson while I was working for him during World War I. I asked the President what effect he believed World War I would have on civilization, and his reply was brief, but it was a masterpiece which you should remember as long as you live.

"I cannot answer your question," said the President, "Because I have no facts on which to base an opinion."

If you will remember Woodrow Wilson's 15-word speech every time you are about to express an opinion about anything, you will soon get out of the habit of expressing or even having opinions based on anything other than proved, observable facts.

Observe people around you carefully and you'll find that the more successful a person is, the less he's inclined to express wild, unjustified opinions about anything.

Also, you probably know drifters, who suffer with frustrations from their many failures, and usually have an assortment of opinions on about everything you can imagine.

Often when I hear someone giving a definite opinion about something that he knows little or nothing, I think of a gentleman and his time piece.

Once I stopped an elderly gentleman and asked him the time. He took out his watch and examined it carefully. Then he replied in an exacting tone of voice, "Well, sir, according to this alleged timepiece, it appears to be approximately one minute and ten seconds past 12:00."

I was particularly impressed by the care with which this man identified the source of his information. Afterwards, I often thought after it how useful it would be if everyone who express opinions or gives out information would take the time to identify the sources where they got their data.

Neither you nor I can influence all people to engage in this sort of safe thinking. But while we are on this subject, just give it a moment – and think what might happen if you could.

RIGHT HERE I CAN GIVE you a simple rule which may help you avoid being misled by unsound opinions others give out.

When you hear someone make a statement which you can't accept as fact-based, or which you question or should question for any reason, ask a simple forward question: "*How do you know?*"

Stand firm on that question and either make the speaker identify the source from which he got his "fact", or let go of the statement entirely as if it had not been made. And do this no matter who is speaking or what may be his reputation for truth and veracity. A statement is fact-based or not, its source is fact-based or not.

Remember, your richest birthright is the privilege of controlling your own thoughts. So treat this divine gift with the profound respect it deserves. Don't allow anyone to do your thinking for you or to influence your thinking in any manner – except by these rules of accurate thinking.

Follow this procedure regardless of what people think or say about your method of thinking. Let them call you what they wish. For your own good, go right on thinking by rules which will save you from many mistakes and tragedies throughout your life.

NOW HERE ARE SEVEN rules to follow that, if you memorize them and follow them as a daily habit, can bring you certainty as an accurate thinker.

> **One**, never accept the opinions of other people as being facts until you have learned the source of those opinions and satisfied yourself of their accuracy.

Two, remember that free advice, no matter from whom it is received, will need the closest of examination before it can be acted on as safe. And, generally speaking, this sort of advice is worth exactly what it you paid for it.

Three, alert yourself immediately when you hear anyone speaking of others in a discourteous or slanderous spirit. This very fact should put you on notice that what you are hearing is biased, to say the very least, and it may be completely erroneous.

Four, in asking others for information, do not disclose to them what you wish the information to be, because most people have the bad habit of trying to please under such circumstances. Well-measured, tactful questions can be of great benefit to you in thinking accurately.

Five, remember that anything which exists anywhere throughout the universe is capable of proof, and where no such proof can be found, it is safer to assume it never existed.

Six, one of the great unexplainable miracles consists in the fact that both truth and falsehood, no matter by what means they may be expressed, carry with them a silent and invisible means of identifying themselves as such. And so, remember this truth and begin developing the necessary intuitive faculty to enable you to sense what is false and what is true.

Seven, follow the habit of asking, "How do you know?" when anyone makes a statement you cannot identify as truth. Follow this habit faithfully, and you will see many persons squirm and turn red in the face when you insist upon a direct reply.

The most accurate thinkers are disciplined, impartial scientists. They investigate with open minds and never allow their wishes to become the fathers of facts but deal with each fact as it is, not as they would like it to be.

Such scientists never align their results to influence their next research funding. (Those latter type of people are not true scientists, regardless of how many degrees they have. Where they are employed, or how long they've held their positions, is also of no account.)

Now, one final word of warning I feel I should leave with you: Study yourself carefully, and you may discover that your own emotions can be your greatest handicap in the business of accurate thinking. It is easy for you to believe that which you *wish* to believe. Unfortunately, that is precisely what most people do.

This is a method many people use to condemn themselves to eternal failure and defeat. And this also condemns them to "reaping the whirlwind" by neglecting to take possession of their minds and use them constructively to attain what they want most in life.

Focused Attention

I'VE NEVER KNOWN OF any successful person in the upper brackets of success. in any calling, that hasn't acquired the great power of concentration upon one thing at a time.

You've heard people speak of others, intending what they say to be derogatory by calling them "people with one-track minds."

Well, anytime anybody says I have a one track mind. I want to thank him for it because there are a lot of people that have multi-track minds and they try to run on all of those tracks at the same time - and don't make a good job on any of them.

I have observed the outstanding successes are people who have developed a high capacity to keep their mind fixed upon one thing at a time. When you have learned to concentrate on one thing at a time, you have learned to key yourself up to where you can see yourself already in possession of the thing that you're concentrating on.

The nine basic motives are the starting point of all concentration. In other words, you don't concentrate unless you have a motive for doing it.

Definiteness of Purpose, of an obsessional proportion, is the "moving spirit" back of any motive. There's no use of having a motive unless you put obsessional desire or obsessional purpose of back of it.

What's the difference between an ordinary purpose or desire and an obsessional desire. What's the difference?

Intention.

In other words, to wish for a thing, or to hope for thing doesn't cause anything to happen. But when you put a burning desire or an obsessional desire in back of the thing, it moves you into action and it attracts you to others and attracts things to you that you need in order to fulfill that desire.

How do you go about developing an obsessional desire about anything?

You select one thing, you eat it, you sleep it, you drink it, you breathe it. You talk about it as long as you can find anybody that will listen - and if you can't find anybody, you talk to yourself.

Repetition. Keep on telling your subconscious mind exactly what you want, make it clear, make it plain, make it definite. And above everything else, let your subconscious mind know that you expect results. And accept no fooling around from it.

An organized endeavor or a personal initiative is the self-starter that starts the action on concentration.

Applied Faith is the sustaining force that keeps action going. In other words, without that applied faith, when the going gets to be hard, that it will no matter what you're doing, you would either slow down or maybe quit. So you can see that you need Applied Faith to keep your action keyed up to a high degree, even when the going is hard - and when the results are not coming in as you would like them to come.

Have you ever heard of anybody starting out to do anything and achieving an outstanding permanent success, right from the start without any opposition? I want to tip you off to the fact that nobody ever did that - and probably nobody ever will. The going is hard, always, with everyone, no matter what you're doing.

Then the *Master Mind* is the source of allied power necessary to ensure success. Can you imagine anybody concentrating on the attainment of something of an outstanding nature without to making use of the

Master Mind - and the brains and the influence and the education of other people? Did you ever hear of anybody achieving an outstanding success without the cooperation of other people?

I have never found anybody yet in the upper brackets of achievement in any line that didn't owe their success, very largely to the friendly, harmonious cooperation of other people. And to the use of other people's brains and sometimes other people's money.

So you need the Master Mind alliance in your concentration. If you're aiming for anything above mediocrity.

Of course you can do your own concentrating on failure. That's why you won't need any help on that. You'll have a lot of volunteer help with it. And a lot of company along well – if you just aim to fail.

But if you're going to succeed, you've got to follow these regulations as I'm laying them down for you. You can't escape them and you can't neglect any one of them.

Self Discipline is the watchman that keeps action moving in the right direction. Even when they're going is difficult. Incidentally, that is where you need self discipline the most. It's when you meet with opposition or when the conditions and circumstances that you've got to cut through are difficult. There is where you'll need yourself discipline to keep your faith going and keep yourself determined that you're not going to quit. Just because the going is hard.

So you couldn't possibly get along in concentrating without self-discipline. Oh, you could, if everything went your way, and then it's no trouble at all. You can concentrate on anything if you don't meet any difficult circumstances.

Creative Vision or *Imagination* is the architect that fashions practical plans for your action back of your concentration. Before you can concentrate intelligently, you've got to have plans, you've got to have an architect. And that architect is your imagination and the imaginations of your Master Mind allies, if you have them. What happens when you start out to do something without a definite practical plan? Did you ever hear of anybody who had a very fine objective ,or very fine purpose, or a very fine idea - but it failed because he didn't have the right kind of a plan for putting it over?

Have you ever heard of any other kind except that? Is that a common pattern? As a matter of fact, for many people have ideas, but the plans for carrying them out are not good, not sound.

Going the Extra Mile is the principal that insures harmonious cooperation from others. You'll need that in the business of a concentration.

To get other people to help you, they'll need you to give them a motive. Even your Master Mind allies that are in your own organization - they won't serve without a motive. And what are some of the motives that would get people to join you in a given undertaking? In all business and professional undertakings, I would say the desire for financial gain is the outstanding motive.

If you're going into a business where the main object is to make money, and if you don't allow your Master Mind allies or your key men and women or the people who are helping you most to get sufficient returns - you're not going to have them very long. They're soon going into business for themselves. They'll be going over to your competitors.

I was very astounded once to hear Mr. Andrew Carnegie tell me that he paid Charlie Schwab, $75,000 a year salary. And on some years, a bonus in addition to his salary of a million dollars. He did that several years. To me, that was a lot of money then, and it's still a lot of money now. Well, I was curious. Again, I wanted to know why a man of his great intelligence would pay one man, like that a bonus of more than 10 times as much as his salary.

And I asked him if he felt he had to do that? He answered, "No, I certainly didn't. I could just let him go out and go into competition with me. Sure. I didn't have to do it."

There's quite a bit of meaning back of that statement. In other words, you got a good man there that was very valuable to him and he wanted to keep him. And he knew that the way to keep him was, to let him know he'd make more money with Mr. Carnegie than he would without him.

The applied *Golden Rule* gives one moral guidance to the actions on what one is concentrating.

Accurate Thinking saves you from daydreaming while you're creating your plans. Most of the so-called "thinking" is nothing in the world but daydreaming or hoping or wishing. There are a lot of people in this world who spend the vast majority of the time, daydreaming and hoping and wishing - "thinking" about things, but never taking any actual physical or mental concrete action in carrying out their plan.

I had an experience a long time ago when I was lecturing over in Des Moines, Iowa, on this philosophy. After the lecture was over, an elderly man tottered up to the stage. He was decrepit and not very strong. Once we met, he fished around in his pocket and came up with a great bundle of papers that had dog-ears on them. As he fished around among those papers, he came up with one on yellow paper. He held it up and said, "This is, nothing new, Mr. Hill. What you just said - I had those ideas 20 years ago."

It was right there on paper. He had those ideas. Sure. And millions of other people had them, too. But nobody did anything about them.

There's nothing new in this philosophy, not a thing new in it, except the law of *natural balance*. That's the only new thing about it. And that's strictly speaking, is not new. That's that's an interpretation of Emerson's essay on Compensation, but stated in terms that people can understand the first time they read it.

Yes, there it was. This man carried those ideas around in his pocket, and he could have been "Napoleon Hill" instead of me – if he only got busy back before I started. One of these days, some smart fellow will come along and he can take up right where I stopped. And he will create a philosophy based on what I've done, that might even be far superior to this.

Learning from each defeat insures one against quitting, when the going get harder. It's a marvelous thing to know that in this philosophy you have learned beyond any question that failure and defeat and adversity needn't stop you - that there's a benefit in every such experience.

CONTROLLED ATTENTION involves the blending and the application of many of the other principles of the philosophy. Persistence should be the watch word behind all of these principles. Controlled attention is the twin brother of definiteness of purpose. Just think what you could do with those two principles. Definiteness of purpose - knowing exactly what you want – to concentrate everything you've got on that one purpose. Do you know what would happen to your mind, your brain and to your whole personality and to yourself, if you would only concentrate on one definite thing?

By concentrating on one definite thing, I mean for you to put all of the time that you can possibly spare when you're not sleeping and not working currently – all of the time that you can possibly spare – seeing yourself in possession of a thing that represents your definiteness of purpose. Seeing yourself in possession of it, seeing yourself building plans, retaining it, working out the first step that you can take. Then the second, and then the third and so on - concentrating on it day in and day out. And in a little while, you'll get to the point that every way you turn, you'll find something in the way of an opportunity that will lead you a little bit closer to the thing that represents your definiteness of purpose.

When you know what you want it, it's astounding how many things you will find that are related to exactly what you want. And you'll accumulate the experiences of people who know what they want and are successful in getting – they don't let anything stop them at all.

No opposition - they just don't pay any attention to opposition. I've often watched Mr. Stone, my distinguished business associate, and listen to his talk to his salesman. I tell you, I get a thrill every time I hear him speak. Cause that man doesn't end it. I don't believe he knows what the word "no" means. I think he's long since believes it means a Yes. That's right. Then the results he gets shows that he means it. He believes it means yes. He can be the most definite about the things he wants of anybody I've ever known. And the most definite in the failure and the refusal to accept a turn down. Now, there were some objects getting his way, he just goes right over them or around them. Or he blows them out of the way, but he never let him stop him. Now that's concentration. That's definiteness of purpose put into action.

Take Henry Ford for instance. Everybody knows what his obsessional definite purpose was. Everybody knows it. Most people have been driving a part of his major purpose around every day of their lives. Driving it. It was a low priced, dependable automobile. And he didn't allow anybody to pitch to him. I have heard promoters approach Mr. Ford, with the opportunities that seemed to me to be most glittering. And his reply always was that he was engaged in the one thing that's consumed all of his time. He was not interested in anything outside of his definite major purpose - which was to make and distributed all over the world, low price, dependable automobiles.

And of course, sticking to that job made him fabulously rich. There were hundreds of people that I saw come into the field and spend more money, infinitely more money than Mr. Ford had to start off with. They went back into the graveyard of failure, and I couldn't find a dozen people in the world who knew what their names were.

These were men who were better educated than Mr. Ford, had better personalities, had everything that he had and a lot more, except one thing - they didn't stick to the very last. They didn't stick to the one definiteness of purpose in the ways that he did, when the going got hard.

Mr. Edison, in the field of invention, was a marvelous illustration of what concentration could do. Where Mr. Edison was a genius in any sense, it was because when the going was hard, then it was there he turned on the most steam - and he didn't quit. Think of a man standing by and keeping on to 10,000 different failures as he did when he was working on the incandescent electric lamp.

Ten thousand. Can you imagine yourself going to 10,000 failures in the same field without wondering if you shouldn't have your head examined? I was so astounded when I heard about that – and even more when I saw his log books. There was two tall stacks of them. Each book held about 250 pages each - and on every page, there was a different plan that he had tried and it had failed.

And I asked him, "Mr. Edison, suppose that you hadn't of found the answer, what would you be doing right now?" He said, "I would be in my laboratory working instead of up here, fooling away my time with you." And I will say on his behalf, he grinned when he said that, but believe you me - he meant just exactly what he was saying.

And signers of the Declaration of Independence and George Washington and Abraham Lincoln. And Thomas Jefferson - his concentration was to give personal liberties to all of the American people and eventually to the people of the world. It may well be freedom for mankind - that, this is the cradle for the birth of the freedom of mankind itself.

Because I know of no other nation on the face of this earth that is concentrating upon the freedom of the individual as we are doing here in the United States. And I know of no other philosophy, no other people engaged in any other studies, whose objective is to free so many people as those who are studying this philosophy.

III – Mindset Habits

———

Pleasing Personality

YOUR PERSONALITY DETERMINES whether people are attracted to you or shy away from you.

It is the show-window in which you display your character to the world, and it is the one thing which distinguishes you from all other human beings.

It is your trademark by which people recognize you, and it is the thing which determines your success or failure in selling yourself through life.

Therefore, you should see your personality just as others see it, so you may improve it where it needs improvement. Your personality consists of more than 30 different factors, traits, and characteristics. Because of the limit of space I can devote in this chapter, I can mention only the more important of your traits of personality.

But before I begin to describe these traits, I want you to know that every trait which goes into your personality is under your control and you can improve it to be whatever you want it to be.

Let's start with the most important trait of your personality: **your mental attitude**. This trait attracts people to you and causes them to like you or repel them and dislike you.

Your mental attitude must be positive to attract people to you.

"How do other people know whether your mental attitude is positive or negative?" you may ask. Well, the answer is easy:

- You disclose this information by the tone of your voice, whether it is pleasant or harsh;

- by the expression on your face, whether it is soft and pleasing or harsh and scowling;

- by the courtesy and consideration you show other people or the lack of these.

People seem to pick up your attitude by telepathy. There is no escape from revealing to others the exact nature of your personality.

The next most important trait of your personality consists of your **flexibility of your mental attitude** or your lack of it. If you have flexibility, you adjust yourself to all the circumstances in your relations with others without losing your composure or allowing yourself to become irritable or angry.

Just remember, if you have flexibility of your mental attitude, it will be impossible for anyone to make you angry or to irritate you without your consent or cooperation.

You cannot control the actions of other people which might justify your irritation with them, but you can control your own reaction by exercising your trait of *flexibility*. And you will observe that all people in the higher brackets of success have this flexibility and they do control their reaction to the influences of other people.

The third most important trait of a pleasing personality is the **ability to control and direct your emotion of enthusiasm**. Enthusiasm is one of the means by which you can give forcefulness to your words. But you must be able to turn it on and off at will as definitely as you can turn on and off water at the spigot. Uncontrolled enthusiasm often makes people tiresome as company. It also may open wide the window to your mind where other people may enter and influence you in ways you don't want.

The fourth most important trait of a pleasing personality is a **sincerity of purpose**. The person who is not sincere in all relationships with others is soon detected and rejected – because no one is attracted to the person who only wants to deceive others. Sincerity is one quality of character which cannot be successfully faked, not even by the most conniving or effective actor. Insincerity carries with it some warning signs which other people recognize. You have only to go back into your own experience with insincere people to prove the truth of what I have stated.

There are 26 other important traits which give you a pleasing personality, but I do not have space to give them to you in this brief chapter.

NOW, LET US TURN OUR attention to some of the common habits which *destroy* a pleasing personality. Please check yourself as I describe these negative habits, and you may make discoveries about yourself that enable you to rebuild your entire personality – so it will become a master salesman on your behalf.

One: one of the most destructive habits which make one's personality objectionable is that of *breaking in and running away with the conversation* when others are speaking.

And **two**, *sarcasm* expressed by insinuations and wisecracks, which are not so wise, is near the head of the list of habits which give one a negative personality.

And **third**, *vanity* expressed by either words or actions is sure to make one unpopular.

And **four**, *indifference* in listening while others are speaking is sure to be noticed and resented. It is more profitable to be a good listener than it is to be a good talker, because one is always apt to learn something while listening to others but never learns anything from hearing himself talk.

Five, the attempt to flatter where *flattery* is obviously not deserved will bring quick resentment from others. Also, it will put them on notice, if they are wise, that the flatterer wants something he perhaps should not get.

And **six**, the habit of *finding fault* with the world at large and people in general is never a popular habit, and it is no part of a pleasing personality. It is far better to direct conversation to the circumstances and things which are right than to complain of those which one believes to be wrong.

And **seven**, one of the very worst habits which destroy a pleasing personality is that of *openly and directly challenging* those with whom one may not agree where there is no obvious reason for doing so except the desire to be on the opposite side.

And **eight**, the habit of *volunteering unsolicited advice* to others who have not requested it can make one an intolerable bore. Free advice usually is considered to be worth just what it costs, which is nothing but the patience with which to listen to it.

And **nine**, the habit of *speaking of one's physical ailments, worries, and personal problems* may be tolerated by others, but this habit will never make one welcome or pleasing. If you wish to make yourself welcome in your relations with others, manage to talk about things which interest and concern those to whom you are speaking. You will never be tiresome to any person if you are speaking of himself and the things which interest him – a truth which all master salesmen understand and respect.

And **ten**, the habit of endeavoring to *convey an impression of superiority* through the use of words and topics unfamiliar to others is a surefire destroyer of popularity. If you wish to sell yourself to others successfully, you must negotiate with them on their own level through terms which they understand.

And **eleven**, *envy* of those who are successful is a trait which destroys a pleasing personality. The truly great men and women have all been known to be generous, sympathetic, and joyous in connection with the good fortunes of others.

And **twelve**, *slovenliness* in body posture and in clothing never attracts but always repels others. "Clothes make not the man", as has been said, but they surely give him a mighty good start if they are appropriate and properly worn. Carelessness in body carriage and posture is immediately traceable to a negative mental attitude.

If you are free from these twelve common habits which make one unpopular, you probably have a very pleasing personality. There are five other negative habits which make one unpopular which I haven't space to cover here.

———————————

REMEMBER THIS, PLEASE: *If you're not liked by other people, you may be sure there is a reason which you can detect and correct.* It is unnatural for one person to dislike another without a cause. Before you can make full use of the earlier principles, you will need to make your personality pleasing. This will require courage, and honesty with yourself.

A pleasing personality stands near the head of the list of assets which make one truly rich. I was impressed with this truth many years ago when I heard Andrew Carnegie say that he paid his right-hand mastermind ally, Charles M. Schwab, $75,000 a year for the services he rendered directly. But he often gave Mr. Schwab a bonus at the end of the year of a million dollars for the influence he exerted on his associate workers because of his pleasing personality.

Andrew Carnegie, who has been said to have been the greatest judge of man this nation has ever known, placed a value on a pleasing personality of more than ten times as much as he valued the personal services of his right-hand man.

Perhaps this will give you a clue that may help you increase the market value of your personality.

Positive Mental Attitude

AS I HAVE SUGGESTED earlier, a positive mental attitude can clear away all obstacles which stand between you and your major purpose in life.

Because of the importance of the subject of this chapter, I won't just tell you that a positive mental attitude heads the entire list of the 12 great riches in life, but I am going to give you explicit instructions as to what you must do to keep your mind positive.

1. LEARN TO ADJUST YOURSELF to other people's state of mind and difficulties so as to get along peacefully with them and to refrain from taking notice of trivial circumstances in your relations with other people by refusing to allow them to become controversial incidents. Great people always avoid small incidents of controversy when possible.

2. ESTABLISH FOR YOURSELF a definite fixed system of conditioning your mind at the beginning of each day so you will keep it positive under all circumstances.

3. LEARN THE ART OF SELLING YOURSELF to other people by indirection, such as asking leading questions which will bring out the sort of reactions from others which you desire. And do not permit yourself to be drawn into argument over unimportant subjects.

4. ADOPT THE HABIT of having a good, hearty laugh every time you become irritated or angry, and it will help you if you begin each day with one minute of hearty laughing. This will change the chemistry of your brain and start you out with a positive mental attitude. (However, you may want to do this in private when you start your laughing exercise.)

5. START EACH DAY with an expression of gratitude for all the adversities, defeats, failures you have experienced in the past. And search for the seed of an equivalent benefit these have yielded you through the passing of time. Then give thanks for the blessings you expect to receive during the day.

6. LEARN TO CONCENTRATE YOUR ATTENTION on the can-do portion of all of your problems and desires and start action where you stand in carrying out this portion. No matter what may be your problem or your desire, there is always something you can do right now that will help you. Find out what this something is and do it.

7. LEARN TO TRANSMUTE all unpleasant circumstances into immediate action which calls for a positive mental attitude, and make this a fixed habit. For example, when you are angry, switch your mind to some sort of action in connection with your hobby or your major purpose in life, and keep it busy with that subject for five minutes.

8. RECOGNIZE THAT EVERY CIRCUMSTANCE which influences your life, whether it is a pleasant or unpleasant circumstance is grist for your mill of life, and so use it to make it pay you dividends in one form or another, remembering meanwhile that your strength grows out of your struggles. Follow this instruction and you will soon learn that there is no such thing as an unprofitable experience.

9. LOOK UPON YOUR LIFE as a continuous process of education of learning from all your experiences, good and bad, and be always on the alert for gains of wisdom which come to you a little at a time in both your pleasant and unpleasant experiences.

10. MAKE THE WORLD OVER to fit your own pattern if you choose – but begin with yourself in some sort of self-improvement which will make you more open-minded, patient, and generous in your relations with others.

11. EXPRESS GRATITUDE twice daily for your recognition of the fact that you have been given complete control over your own mind, and ask for guidance in order that you may use this profound gift wisely in all your thoughts and acts.

12. GO OUT OF YOUR WAY daily to comment enthusiastically on the good qualities of those with whom you live and work, but do not mention their negative qualities. Then, observe as benefit to yourself how quickly others will begin to concentrate on your good qualities. Remember, I'm still talking about how to keep your mind positive.

13. ACCEPT ALL CRITICISM of yourself as an occasion for self-examination to determine how much of it is justified and you will be sure to make startling discoveries about yourself which will help you through the remainder of your life.

14. DO NOT ACCEPT FROM LIFE or anyone else anything you do not desire, and remember that Mahatma Gandhi proved himself to be more powerful than the great British military forces by this simple method of passive resistance.

15. REMEMBER ALWAYS that there are only two kinds of circumstances which cause you to worry: those you can do something about, and those you can do nothing about. Nothing, that is, except to use passive resistance, and refuse to permit them to worry you.

16. KEEP YOUR MIND always and only engaged in thinking about that which you desire most, your major purpose in life. Waste no time on thinking about that you do not want.

17. IF YOU SHOULD EVER find yourself "feeling sorry" for yourself, look around until you find someone who is worse off than yourself and start right there to give him help. Make this procedure a habit and you will witness one of the great miracles of life, because that which you do to or for another you do to or for yourself.

18. CHOOSE SOME PERSON whom you consider to be the sort of person you would like to be, then start emulating that person in every way possible. Great people have always been hero worshipers, but they pick the right sort of people to emulate.

19. CULTIVATE YOUR TONE OF VOICE so that your words have a pleasing, musical sound, and remember that the sound of your voice is an open window through which other people look into your very soul. It will be a profitable investment if you will get a tape recording machine and record samples of your voice daily while you practice the art of expressing yourself through a friendly sounding voice. If you are engaged in selling, this practice will quickly pay off in monetary dividends.

20. Last, but by no means the least, WRITE OUT THIS SENTENCE and paste it in a prominent place where you work and on a mirror where you see yourself in your home:

> "Whatever the mind can conceive and believe the mind can achieve."

The 20 instructions I have just given you have come from my own personal experiences over more than 50 years, and they represent also my observations of more than 500 successful people who helped me to organize the Science of Success philosophy.

I claim no copyright on these great truths, and I want you to possess them because I know they can bless you the remainder of your life if you are ready to accept them and to put them into action.

Remember also that you are the only person who can provide you with a positive mental attitude. What are you going to do about it?

On your answer to this question rests your entire future.

Personal Initiative

PERSONAL INITIATIVE is the dynamo which starts the faculty of imagination into action in the process of translating one's definite major purpose into its physical or financial equivalent.

If you aim for success above mediocrity, you will need to learn to act on your own personal initiative, because your success is something which you must achieve for yourself – without someone telling you what to do or how to do it.

Cyrus H. K. Curtis, the former owner of "The Saturday Evening Post," and one of my collaborators in organizing the science of success philosophy, was responsible distilling a key motto on personal imitative I want you to have:

> *"There are two kinds of men who never amount to much: those who cannot do as they are told, and those who can do nothing else."*

Of course, Mr. Curtis's implication is very clear. He implied that those who amount to something worthwhile in life are those who move on their own personal initiative without being told what to do or why they should do it. The men who stand out in the minds of the public as the greatest successes, from the days of George Washington on to the present, are those who chose their own occupation, business, or profession – and moved on their own personal initiative in achieving their purpose.

And those who are getting ahead most rapidly today, no matter in what position they began, are those who promote themselves to a higher place in life by acting on their own personal initiative.

THE HABIT OF PERSONAL imitative not only inspires one to move on his own responsibility, but it also influences him to carry through until he completes what he undertakes in a manner pleasing to all concerned, because he knows that "a winner never quits and a quitter never wins."

And right here is an appropriate place to say that *a big success is made up of a great number of little circumstances.* Each of which is so small and seemingly insignificant that most people pass it by as not worthy of notice.

Some may think, for example, that the habit of personal initiative is unimportant. But we have only to take a look at the record of some of our greatest successes to recognize that personal initiative was an important factor that without it, they never would have achieved success.

For example, no one told F. W. Woolworth to start a five and ten-cent store. The idea was his own. He acted on his own personal initiative in putting his idea to action and lived to see it yield him a fortune well above $100 million.

W. Clement Stone started his insurance business on his own personal initiative with an operating capital of only $100. But he followed through on that same personal initiative and made his humble beginning yield an annual gross income of many millions of dollars.

And it was that same habit of acting on his own personal initiative, of doing the thing he wanted to do, which inspired Mr. Stone to join forces with me in taking the Science of Success philosophy to millions of people throughout the world. This undertaking is believed may help more people to find their places in the world than has any other influence during the past hundred years.

THE HABIT OF PERSONAL initiative was the chief trait which helped Henry J. Kaiser to build a great industrial empire and raise himself to a high position in the industrial world. It was this trait of personal initiative which inspired Mr. Kaiser to pile up such an enormous record in the building of ships during World War II, despite the fact that he had never built ships before.

One day, when I was lecturing to one of my classes, I mentioned Henry J. Kaiser's wonderful record in building ships more cheaply and quickly than experienced shipbuilders had been able to do, when one of my students spoke up and said, "Mr. Kaiser's being a friend of Jesse Jones of the Federal Reserve Bank didn't hurt his chances of success any, did it?"

Well, for a moment, it looked as if that question had placed me on a spot. But I soon recovered my composure and came back with this reply. "No, his knowing Mr. Jones did not hurt his chances, but think of the thousands of industrialists, many of whom also knew of Mr. Jones, but did not use their personal initiative in getting his financial help."

Personal initiative is one quality which inspires a person to form friendships and make contacts with people who can assist them in times of need. It was my personal initiative which influenced Andrew Carnegie to give me an opportunity to organize the Science of Success philosophy.

———

HERE'S AN OUTLINE OF the more important attributes of a person who has enough personal initiative to become the leader in his chosen field:

> **One:** first of all, the person who follows the habit of personal initiative has a *definite major purpose in life and a plan for its attainment.*

Two: and a *mastermind alliance* with those whose help is essential in achieving his major purpose.

Three: he has the necessary *persistence,* and the will to win, that carries him along when the going is hard and he meets with obstacles.

Four: he *makes decisions promptly* when he has the necessary facts on which to base them and changes them slowly, if at all.

Five: he follows the habit of *doing more than he is paid for,* and he does so in a pleasing, *positive mental attitude.*

Six: he *accepts full responsibility* for everything he undertakes and never passes the buck when things go wrong.

Seven: he takes *friendly criticism without resentment* because he has learned to profit by it.

Eight: he knows t*he nine basic motives are which inspire all human endeavors* and never requests anyone to do anything for him without giving that person an adequate motive for doing so.

Nine: he only expresses an opinion about anything once he's thought the subject through – and is prepared to state how he came by his opinion.

Ten: he follows the habit of listening much and talking only when he has something to say that benefits others.

Eleven: he has a *well-developed sense of observation of small details* and knows his job from the smallest detail to the greatest.

Twelve: he never tells anyone to do anything without suggesting why it should be done and how it may be done best.

Thirteen: he follows the habit of *concentrating his full attention on one thing at a time.*

Fourteen: his mental attitude is positive at all times when he is in communication with other people.

Fifteen: if you ask him a question, he will give you a direct answer, even if he has to tell you he does not know the correct answer.

Sixteen: last, but perhaps most important of all, *he never puts off until tomorrow that which should have been done last week,* because he knows that the habit of procrastination is near the top of the list of the causes of failure.

If you can rate okay on each of these sixteen traits of personal initiative, you are a leader in your field of endeavor. When you come to examine yourself on the subject of personal initiative, just remember that your success or your failure depends very largely on the action you take in connection with your occupation.

No one will tell you what you should do. No one will tell you what not to do. The decision must be your own and you must follow through and carry out your decision on your own personal initiative.

If you work for wages or a salary, you should decide to promote yourself through your own personal initiative to the top of the scale in your occupation. And remember that your promotion is entirely in your hands.

UP TO THIS POINT, I've given you a blueprint of the steps you should take in promoting yourself to whatever station in life you desire.

Now, let me give you a brief review of five principles we have covered previously.

> **One**: *definiteness of purpose*. By now you should know what you want most from life and you should have a plan for getting it. Here is the most important circumstance of your whole life where you must move on your own personal initiative, because no one else can tell you what you should want most.

> **Two**: *the mastermind principle*. If you have not already formed a friendly alliance with those who can help you in attaining your major purpose in life, you should move on your own personal initiative and form this alliance at once.

> **Three**: *applied faith*. This is the principle which gives you power in carrying out your definite major purpose and all minor purposes.

> **Four**: *going the extra mile*. This is a must if your major purpose is anything above mediocrity.

> **Five**: *a pleasing personality* is an asset of priceless value, and it, too, is something you must acquire through your personal initiative.

You see, then, that personal initiative enters into every one of the success principles. And as you continue studying the complete system of 17 Science of Success Principles, you'll also find that these principles each build and interact with previous and later principles – all to help you arrive at the goal you've selected to achieve.

Enthusiasm

THE SUBJECT OF ENTHUSIASM may be likened to steam in a boiler of an ocean liner which, when it is turned on and controlled, starts the massive turbines and propellers to put the ship into motion, and power all shipboard functions – all to safely deliver thousands of occupants safely to their destination near and far across the vast oceans.

Someone has said that knowledge is power. That is only a half-truth, for knowledge generates power only when it is put into action for the attainment of a definite objective.

Enthusiasm is one of the more powerful means by which we may put into action our education, experience, and knowledge. Spoken words without enthusiasm are often ineffective, and sometimes they can actually sound boring. You've no doubt noticed the effect a speaker without enthusiasm has on his listeners.

I have known lecturers to hold audiences spellbound for two hours. Yet, when members of the audience were asked to tell what the speaker had said, they could not remember. But what they did remember was that the speaker got their attention and held it.

Here's why enthusiasm has such a powerful impact upon the minds of those who come under its influence: Your brain and every other person's brain is both a broadcasting station and a receiving station which sends out thought vibrations and picks up those sent out by other people.

When you turn on your enthusiasm, you step up the vibrations of thoughts which go out from your brain so that they reach and affect other people more quickly.

Known to psychologists for ages, it is also known to most master salesmen who use this to condition the minds of their prospective buyers before they ever talk with them. You have probably seen for yourself that enthusiasm is very contagious, that it engages the attention of those who come under its influence, and that it causes listeners to respond in a similar spirit of enthusiasm.

I once heard Andrew Carnegie say that, "If you turn loose one man who thought in terms of intense enthusiasm in an industrial plant employing thousands of people, this man's enthusiasm would very quickly reach and influence every person in the plant."

And he said it made no difference whether the enthusiasm was negative or positive, constructive or destructive. Carnegie went on to explain that in his selection of employees for promotion to bigger jobs, the first thing he looked for was a man's capacity to express himself in terms of intense enthusiasm. He said that enthusiasm is one of the most important traits necessary for leadership.

The most successful lawyers are not necessarily those who know most about the legal profession, but they are those who know how to influence courts and juries – through their belief in their cases and their great capacity for expressing themselves with enthusiasm.

When you are introduced to another person, you have a marvelous opportunity to sell yourself favorably to that person with your expressed enthusiasm.

When you shake hands with another person, you have also a fine opportunity to make a good impression by the warmth of enthusiasm you put into that handshake. If there is anything which leaves me flat and unfavorably impressed when I'm introduced, it's an extended hand which feels like a piece of cold ham and acknowledges the introduction with a cold, canned, "Pleased to meet you..." with no signs of enthusiasm back of it.

Right here, let me give you a brief course in salesmanship that can help you the rest of your life. When you meet anyone on whom you which to make a favorable impression, when it is someone you haven't previously met or even someone already have, do these things:

One – turn on your enthusiasm and so modulate your voice with it so that you definitely make the other person feel you are happy talking with him.

Two – when you shake his hand, take a firm grip on it and give it a quick, firm squeeze at the end of each word you express in your greetings. For example, say, "How are you doing today? I am so very glad to meet you." Do not crush the hand, however, as I have known some people to do.

Three – then, if you begin the conversation, be sure that you direct it to some subject of interest to the other person.

And **four** – follow through by eagerly asking questions which will keep attention focused upon the other person.

Then when you are ready to have the other person hear what you have to say about yourself or your interests or your business, they will have been prepared to listen attentively.

For many years, I taught master salesmanship, and the first important thing I endeavored to teach my students was the importance of *one*: speaking with enthusiasm, and *two*: selling the prospective buyer on himself personally before trying to sell him anything else.

I've often told my students of salesmanship that the best possible way for one to sell himself to others is to first sell the others on themselves.

That counsel was sound when I began training salesmen over 30 years ago, and it is still sound.

When I was a youngster in school, I discovered that the teachers from whom I learned the most were those who expressed the greatest enthusiasm in their teaching.

I have heard an experienced doctor say that the enthusiasm he carries into the sick room with him has more to do with helping to bring about a cure than all the medicine he can prescribe.

———————

AND LET ME GIVE YOU another interesting sidelight on the effects of enthusiasm. I have noticed that enthusiasm not only influences others who come under its effect, but it also very distinctly influences and benefits those who make a habit of expressing it in their thoughts and deeds.

Enthusiasm is an expression of a positive mental attitude, and it has long been known to doctors that a positive mental attitude stands high on the list of influences which give one sound health.

I have heard it said, for example, that only one thing causes stomach ulcers, and that is worry or a negative mental attitude.

And only one thing can cure stomach ulcers, which is a positive mental attitude.

It seems that disease germs cannot live and thrive in the bloodstream of one whose mind is always positive.

———————

I HAVE STILL ANOTHER very important observation concerning the power of enthusiasm: I have observed that prayers expressed with intense enthusiasm bring much quicker and more satisfactory results.

Now, you can try this for yourself and be convinced. I began experimenting with this idea many years ago, and from my experiences, I gathered the information which caused me to change my method of prayer entirely. I now use the prayer I recommended to you earlier with gratifying results. I get quicker and more favorable action from my prayers than I did when I expressed them in a spirit which lacked enthusiasm.

A VERY PRACTICAL WAY to begin learning to express yourself with enthusiasm is to get in the habit of reading aloud for ten minutes daily – putting all the enthusiasm at your command into your reading. You will be surprised in a short while at how much this will help you in speaking with enthusiasm in your ordinary conversations.

If you follow my suggestion that you read aloud for ten minutes daily as a means of acquiring the habit of enthusiasm, I recommend that you write down a list of ten subjects, things, or circumstances in which you have the keenest interest and use this list to select your reading materials. You will have no difficulty in reading in a tone of enthusiasm in connection with the things that you like best.

I would suggest also that you adopt the habit of practicing enthusiasm in your conversations with your family and your business associates. This habit will make you more popular with those who are close to you.

AND FINALLY, LET ME give you an example which gives an interesting cue. You'll perhaps remember when you were courting the person of your choice, or being courted, as the case may be, no one had to tell you how or why to be enthusiastic. Of course not – because the motive of love, or affection, took care of this without effort on your part.

Just remember that enthusiasm is always easily expressed when one is inspired by a burning desire for something or any motive associated with one's closest interests. Where there is no motive, there is apt to be no enthusiasm.

Try the habit of moving with enthusiasm in all of your daily work and... see how much better you will feel.

Going the Extra Mile

THIS SUCCESS PRINCIPLE has marked the turning point of every person who has moved from the lower brackets of success to the higher planes of achievement – where a person acquires *everything* they desire.

This principle is called "The Habit of Going the Extra Mile," which means the habit of rendering *more* service and *better* service than one is expected to render, and doing it with a positive mental attitude.

I'm going to tell you all I know about this magic principle of self-advancement – because it is the one rule you *must* follow if you expect to write your own price tag and be sure of getting it.

Let me describe this success principle for you in a brief formula which you can easily remember. I call it the "QQMA" formula, which means the *quality* of service you render plus the *quantity* of service you render plus the *mental attitude* in which you render service determines the space you occupy in your chosen position and the compensation you get from your services.

If you will examine carefully the people whom you know to be unusually successful, you will discover that they follow the QQMA formula, although they may do so unconsciously.

You can get a big advantage over those who follow this formula unconsciously. And when you make use of it deliberately with purpose and forethought, you can make the principle pay off in a big way and quickly.

———————

HERE'S SOME OF THE benefits you will enjoy by following the habit of going the extra mile.

One, this habit will bring you to the favorable attention of those who can and will provide you with opportunities to promote yourself into a better circumstance.

Two, it will place back of you that great natural law of increasing returns through which the service you render will bring back greater than average compensations.

And **three**, following this habit will make you indispensable in your chosen occupation or calling. Therefore it will place you in a position to write your own ticket.

And **four**, this habit will help you to excel in your line of work, because each time you render service, you endeavor to do a better job than you did previously.

And **five**, if you work for a salary or wages, this habit will give you preference when work is slack and others are laid off.

And **six**, it will help you to benefit by the law of contrast, because the others around you will not be going the first mile, let alone the second mile.

And **seven**, following this habit of doing your very best in all of your efforts and doing it in a pleasing mental attitude will improve your personality and make you liked by others.

And **eight**, it will also help you to develop a keen alert imagination, because you will be continuously seeking new and better ways of rendering useful service.

Nine, it will inspire you to move on your own personal initiative instead of waiting to be told what to do, a habit which is the first step in leadership in all callings.

Ten - The habit of going the extra mile definitely develops greater self-reliance and gives one more courage to move ahead without the fear of criticism from others.

Eleven - it helps you to master the destructive habit of procrastination, the one habit which heads the list of causes of failure.

Twelve, going the extra mile influences other people to respect your integrity, and inspires them to go out of their way to cooperate with you in a friendly spirit.

And **Thirteen**, this habit helps you to develop definiteness of purpose, which is the starting point of all personal success. And it stops you from drifting through life without knowing what you want or where you are going.

And **Fourteen**, here is the grand payoff which this habit gives you. It provides you with the one and only excuse for asking for a promotion to a better station in life or a higher pay. Obviously if you are doing no more than you are being paid for, then you are receiving the exact pay you're entitled to, and you have not a single excuse for asking for more pay or a better position. Simple.

Fifteen, last but not least, the habit of going the extra mile conditions your mind to maintain a mastermind alliance with others.

Every so often I hear people complain about their not receiving favorable breaks in their relations with others. I never hear this sort of complaint from one of my students of the Science of Success course, nor from anyone who has read any book that I have written, because all of my students have learned the secret of how to create their *own* favorable breaks. They do it by following the habit of going the extra mile.

I can tell you frankly, I have never received a major favorable break during my entire life that did not come from having applied the principle of going the extra mile. Sometimes I hear people complain also that their positions are such that they are not permitted to go the extra mile. And my counsel to these people is always the same: change positions and market your services where it pays to go the extra mile. I am sincere in giving this advice because I know that no one can do better than earn a mere living unless and until he begins going the extra mile.

The reason I know definitely that the habit of going the extra mile is a sound procedure is the fact that I have checked this principle as I did all of the other success principles listed in this book to make sure they were in harmony with natural laws.

———————————

I CAN GIVE YOU A FINE example of how nature forces man to go the extra mile in order that he may produce the food with which to exist:

The farmer, for example, must follow the habit of clearing the ground, fencing it, cultivating it, and planting the seed at the right season of the year, all of which he must do in advance – without compensation of any kind. If he does his part of the work properly, he then hands the job over to Nature, sits down, and waits for her to do her part.

And, within a brief period, Nature germinates the seed the farmer plants, matures it, and yields back to him the seed he planted – plus perhaps an increase of a hundred times that amount, just to compensate him for having gone the extra mile.

So we see that the law of increasing returns comes to the aid of the man who goes the extra mile, and this principle applies the same in rendering service on a job as it does in the fields of a farmer.

If farmers didn't follow the habit of going the extra mile, the human race itself would starve to death in one growing season, and I am sure you will agree that any time we can copy Mother Nature's habits, we will not go wrong in doing so.

You now have the possession of the fourth principle of individual achievement.

I am going to offer you three suggestions which may bring you such overwhelming success that you could stop with just these four principles:

> **First**, start now, in whatever occupation you are engaged, to render some form of useful service to someone near you which you are not expected to render and for which you neither expect nor ask for compensation.

> And **two**, render this service in a pleasing mental attitude, which will show clearer that you enjoy doing it.

> And **three**, follow this practice seven days in succession, and then notice what a changed atmosphere you will enjoy in your association with those nearest you.

In carrying out these instructions, do not make known your plan to anyone, but go ahead and do it in the most natural way possible. By the end of the seventh day, you will find yourself so much happier and so much better liked by those around you – that you will never desire to give up the habit.

IV - Vision & Team

Creative Vision

CREATIVE VISION IS the success principle which is responsible for building of all of our plans, aims, and purposes.

It has been said that the *imagination is the workshop where we fashion the purposes of our brain and the ideas of our soul.* I do not know of a better definition of imagination than this.

There are two forms of imagination.

First, there is *synthetic* imagination, which consists of organizing and putting together of recognized ideas, concepts, and facts arranged in a new combination. Very seldom does anyone create an idea or anything else absolutely new. Nearly everything known to civilization is just a re-combination of something that is old.

Secondly, there is *creative* imagination, which operates through the sixth sense and has its base in the subconscious section of the brain and serves as the exclusive medium through which basically new ideas or facts are revealed.

———————————

LET ME GIVE YOU SOME examples of synthetic imagination in action.

One: Edison's invention of the incandescent electric lamp was the creation of synthetic imagination because it was created by bringing together in a new combination two old and well-known principles.

Two: Clarence Saunders's idea that the developed the modern self-serve store system across the globe was based was the result of synthetic imagination because he merely borrowed the self-serve plan used in cafeterias and introduced it into the grocery store business. But despite the simplicity of the plan, it is said to have yielded its organizer $4 million during the first four years after it was put to work in his Piggly-Wiggly store chains.

Three: Henry Ford's first automobile was created through synthetic imagination by the simple procedure of bringing together the well-known method of transportation, the horse and buggy, and the steam-propelled threshing machine. Both ideas were old, but it remained for Henry Ford to combine them in a new method of use and he made himself the most distinguished industrialist of his era by his achievement, not to mention a fabulous fortune.

Four: the man who dipped a hunk of ice cream in chocolate, placed a stick in it for a handle and called it "Eskimo Pie" used synthetic imagination and started a new industry which still has a widespread outlet and grosses a huge sum every year. It is safe to assume that the creator of this simple plan of merchandising was well compensated for his use of his synthetic imagination.

Five: F.W. Woolworth made use of synthetic imagination by the simple procedure of setting up a retail store in which a large variety of merchandise, retailing at 5 and 10 cents per item, was offered to the public and lived to see his merchandising innovation start a series of similar retail stores which gross annually many millions of dollars in sales and made Woolworth rich in the bargain.

NOW SOME EXAMPLES OF creative imagination:

One: Edison's invention of the phonograph was the outgrowth of creative imagination because no part of his invention had ever been known or used previously.

Two: Signor Marconi's invention of wireless communication was also the outgrowth of creative imagination because it was based on basically new ideas which never had been used previously. He was the first to discover the means by which the ether could be made to take the place of wires in the transmission of sound.

Three: Madame Curie's discovery of radium was also the outgrowth of creative imagination because no one before her had ever revealed either the actual existence of radium or the method by which it could be recovered or refined.

Four: Wilbur and Orville Wright's perfection of the modern airplane was a hybrid result of creative imagination and synthetic imagination. Because others, previous to their time, had discovered some of the ideas they used successfully, but they were the first to coordinate those ideas so they worked.

Five: Robert G. LeTourneau made effective use of creative imagination by building heavy dirt-removing machinery which involved ideas never before used, although he was practically unskilled in engineering and had very little schooling of any kind. I worked with Mr. LeTourneau for a year and a half, during which I saw him in action many times when he was drawing entirely upon the faculty of creative imagination and receiving his ideas from sources outside of his own immediate education or knowledge.

I could give you some suggestions as to how you may be able to make profitable use of your imagination, keeping in mind that the faculty of your imagination, like every other faculty of your mind, becomes stale through disuse and alert through use.

In case you have not already recognized this fact – I am bringing you very near the point where people sometimes tune in on their creative imagination and come up with ideas which benefit great numbers of people and make themselves popular and rich.

I've given you these suggestions solely as inspiration intended to introduce you to your inborn faculty of creative imagination.

Imagination is a trait which becomes alert only by constant action based on the success principles I have described above.

You are the one who must supply this action.

Cooperation & Teamwork

THERE ARE TWO KINDS of cooperation, one based upon force or coercion. And the other is a voluntary based upon voluntary action founded on motive.

The vast majority of all circumstances of cooperation are based upon some form of force or coercion. Employees often cooperate with their employer, but there's a certain amount of coercion needed, a certain amount of fear that if they don't cooperate, they'll not have their jobs.

There are other circumstances where the employees cooperate with the employer because the employer has made it so beneficial for them to work at that place, that they do it willingly.

Any kind of cooperation that's forced or forced on people or based upon any type of coercion is not desirable - because people only cooperate on that basis as long as they have to. And when the get to the point where they don't have to do it any longer, they kick over the traces. Relatively speaking, there is a small percentage of employers throughout the United States who understand the advantage of having their employees cooperating with them on a willing basis of friendliness based upon benefits as they extend to those employees.

Cooperation is different from the mastermind principle in that it's based upon coordination of effort without necessarily involving the principle of definiteness of purpose - or the principle of harmony. The men working in the military service - an army of men, for instance, working under their superior officers - represents a tremendous amount of power based upon cooperation, but it doesn't necessarily mean that there's harmony or that they like what they're doing. There's a certain amount of coercion and force there. They're doing what they have to do. Sometimes they like to do it, but sometimes they don't like to do it.

Cooperation based on the mastermind principle is the medium by which great personal power may be attained. No one has ever acquired such power without the aid of these principles. A fact which places them in the category of Indispensable Natural Principles.

Cooperation is indispensable in four major relationships. And here they are:

- in the home,

- in one's job or profession,

- in social relationships, and

- in support of our form of government and free enterprise.

Certainly those are musts. And if every citizen cooperated in those four respects, this would be a better country than we have yet. Now here are examples of cooperation, not based on the mastermind principle: soldiers working under army regulations, employees working under the rules of employment, government officials, working under laws of the nation, professional men (such as lawyers, doctors, and dentists) working under the rules of ethics of their professions, citizens of a nation relegated under a dictator.

Observe that the matter in which the cooperative effort assumes greater power is when the principle of cooperation is combined with the mastermind principle involving harmony based on a definite motive.

You don't do anything in this world without a motive. There must be a motive for everything that you do or everything you refrain from doing. The only person that does things without a motive is an insane person. He doesn't have to have a motive.

Well, first: *the opportunity to get increased compensation and promotion* is one of the most outstanding motives for gaining friendly cooperation. And wherever that has been put into use in any business that I know anything about, there has always been a very beneficial and a very profitable return.

Recognition for personal initiative, pleasing personality and outstanding work. Now that's a strong motive to inspire cooperation. Giving person recognition: when he does a good job, then say so - do something about it.

I know an employer who has the birthdays of all, of the wives of his employees, and all of their children. And every birthday, they all get presents from him. With the cards signed by him, in person. Well, his organization represents just one great big family. He has built himself up in the hearts of the people in the home where the man works. And you can just imagine what that does to the man himself.

And then the third - *taking a personal interest in one's private problems.* You know, that's a powerful motive too, for gaining friendly cooperation, taking an interest in the problems of the people that you're associated with - or that you're working with. Helping them solve problems. You know, a lot of people say, "Oh, well, after all, my problems are mine, but the other fellah's problems are his. I don't know. I'm not interested in that." And you've got the right to do that if you want to, but it won't be profitable to you. Won't be beneficial. If you want to have a lot of friends, you want to have a lot of cooperation. You will make it your business to look around and wherever you can be of help to people, you will start right in being of help to them.

Next, *a system of friendly competition* between departments and in departments between individuals. This is a system of friendly cooperation. Now in a sales organization, for instance, you can have a different group competing with other groups in the same organization on a friendly basis. They all strive to do their best to win, because of good sportsmanship. and able sales managers very often set up that kind of a motive to inspire their sales people to do better jobs.

Then: *the hope of future benefits in the form of some yet unattained goal,* which can best be attained by mutual cooperation. In other words, something that you want to accomplish with a group of people where it can only be accomplished by your all pulling together, in the same direction, at the same time, in the spirit of harmony.

Well, you could mention other motives. There may be in your particular case, you need the cooperation of somebody. Maybe you would know what kind of a motive that you could plant in the mind of that person to get that cooperation. But certainly you can't get it by force or coercion and hope to benefit by it. Because if you get it by that method, sooner or later, the cooperation will play out - and it'll turn into resentment.

Our American system of free enterprise gets friendly cooperation - when it is not interfered with by outside influences - by the profit motive. In the United States, if we took away the profit motive, it would take the very warp and the woof of our whole system of free enterprise away. And there are certain pressure groups that are trying to do that very thing all the time - to take away the profit motive.

You have to have a motive for everything you do. And we have, we believe in the United States and our system of free enterprise, the finest combination of motives that exist anywhere in the world.

Learning From Adversity

NOW WE COME ONTO ONE of the strangest of the 17 principles of success.

This principle which makes it possible for you to meet every adversity, every disappointment, every defeat, and every failure you meet with from now on – for the remainder of your life – and turn these into forward progress toward your definite purpose.

The principle of learning from adversity makes it possible for you to transmute all your past failures and mistakes into an asset which will help you achieve outstanding success in the future.

Your positive mental attitude is the only means to may convert adversities, defeats, and failures into assets.

It seems that everyone should experience adversities, defeats, and even failures as if part of Nature's method of disciplining people to learn how to take possession of their own minds.

Despite the benefits which we may get from adversities and unpleasant experiences of every nature, no one desires to meet with these experiences. A failure or defeat is just as unpleasant to me now as it was 50-odd years ago when I was learning about failures and unpleasant experiences in the great university of hard knocks.

To be truthful, I have to tell you that my greatest blessings in life ultimately resulted from my greatest adversities.

But these blessings never would have been recognized by me if I had not learned this truth: *that every adversity carries with it the seed of an equivalent benefit.* Once you learn that adversities can be made to pay dividends, you will acquire the habit of looking for that seed of an equivalent benefit in each such experience with which you'll meet.

————————

MY FIRST ILLUSTRATION concerns a man of whom you may have heard, and I have no doubt you may have eaten some of the food which he produced and marketed throughout the nation – all as the result of an adversity which would have stopped most men cold.

The man was Milo C. Jones, who owned a small farm near Fort Atkinson, Wisconsin, on which he made only a fair living until he was stricken down with double paralysis, which deprived him of every portion of his body except his brain. In this hour of his greatest adversity, Milo C. Jones used his mind. Took possession of it for the first time in his life perhaps. And out of that mind came the idea of raising hogs and converting them into Little Pig Sausage. And on that same farm where, previous to that adversity, he made only a mere living, he found the seed of an equivalent benefit that compensated him for the loss of the use of his body and lived to see Little Pig Sausage yield him a huge fortune.

Isn't it strange that so often people have to be cut down by failure and defeat before they learn they have minds capable of mastering all of their problems? Isn't it strange why Milo C. Jones did not discover the Little Pig Sausage idea while he had a sound body?

You may find in your adversities the necessary challenge to inspire you on to success such as you never would have known without these experiences. I do not suggest that you look for adversities or expect to meet with them. But if you do so, just remember not to fear them.

And instead of brooding over them, as most people do, let me suggest that you be different and convert them into stepping stones on which you may rise to whatever place in life you have set for yourself.

You can do this by the simple process of appropriating and putting to your use the ten success principles I have given you previously.

Right here, recall the great importance of following the principle of a positive mental attitude. Because this is principle you will need most in converting unpleasant experiences into assets.

———————

MY NEXT ILLUSTRATION involves a very intimate, personal experience of my own which began when my mother passed on. I was eight years of age. I know that the loss of one's mother at any age usually is regarded as an irreparable loss which offers no possible benefits. But even in the loss of loved ones, we may find that there is a seed of an equivalent benefit.

I found that seed in one of the most wonderful persons I have ever known – when my father brought home my new mother. It was she who inspired me to prepare myself for the opportunity of my meeting with Andrew Carnegie. That was where I received the commission to organize the world's first practical philosophy of personal success.

Had it not been for the loss of my mother, you would not be reading this, and my books would not now be serving to help millions of people throughout the world to find their places in life.

———————

JUST REMEMBER THIS about adversities. Nothing is ever so bad or so unpleasant that it may not yield some benefit – *if* we keep a positive mental attitude toward the experience and make it a habit to look for that seed of an equivalent benefit.

This, of course, involves the application of that important success principle, personal initiative.

Our great American way of life, and all the personal freedom and opportunities we enjoy under our way of life, began with our defeat of the British in 1778. Probably every Britisher believed that the loss of the American colonies was an irreparable loss which offered no possible benefits. Yet you and I know that if we had not defeated the British and made ourselves rich and powerful, the British Empire probably would have been wiped out in World Wars I or II. We know also that although the British Empire survived those two wars, it was our financial help which saved the British from starvation and bankruptcy. So, today, every Britisher should give thanks for the defeat of Lord Cornwallis's armies because that defeat finally became the means of survival of the British Empire.

THERE IS A CURRENT and long-standing world trend that still contains an adversity that has yet to be resolved into a seed of an equivalent benefit. There is an ongoing trend in this and all other countries to rob individuals of their rights of personal freedom. There are active factions who are devoted entirely to this trend.

This emerging trend is in direct violation of the obvious purpose of the Creator to give every individual the privilege of freedom of thought and action. There is something definite you and I can do against this ongoing trend to rob us of our rights of personal freedom. We may not be able to turn it back entirely by our individual efforts, but we can and we should do something about it where it affects us individually, as we can know what actions we can take, and how we can go about them.

Of course, you will ask, "What can I do to influence a world trend?" And I will answer by saying there is something definite that you can do. You can refuse to accept this diverging trend and take full possession of your own mind, thus fulfilling your personal responsibility to your Creator.

Remember those two sealed envelopes I mentioned in a previous chapter? One of them is labeled, "Riches You May Enjoy by Taking Possession of Your Own Mind." You have a responsibility to yourself, your loved ones, your Creator, to take possession of your own mind and to direct it to ends of your own choice.

This responsibility is yours, and no one else can rob you of it or fulfill it for you.

You also have a responsibility to your country which has given you our great American way of life, our great system of free enterprise. One so designed to provide everyone with the ability to take possession of his own mind – and writing his own ticket in life.

We should remember that our benefits under the American way of life, like every other blessing we have, was given at birth. And this is something that we can retain and enjoy *only* by making the fullest and best use of it.

It is definitely a part of the overall plan of the universe to give man the benefit only of those blessings he recognizes, embraces, and uses constructively. Tie your arm to your side and take it out of use and nature rebels immediately by causing the arm to atrophy, wither, and become useless. Neglect to keep in contact with your friends, and to cultivate them, and you lose them. Show indifference to the patrons who help you earn your living, or the employer who pays your wages, and very soon you find yourself without a market for your services.

It is an inevitable law of nature that you lose that which you do not use.

Of course, this also applies to the use of your own mind the same as to everything else.

While we so often boast that we are citizens of the richest, the greatest, and the most powerful nation civilization has yet produced, we will do well to remember this law where we lose that which we do not properly use.

IF YOU ARE READY FOR this principle, you will embrace it at once. From here on out, you will know to never sit and brood over unpleasant experiences without knowing full well that your efforts could be better used by searching for that seed of an equivalent benefit which is available in those experiences.

As an assignment: Go back into your past experiences, study each adversity and failure you may have experienced. Look for that seed of an equivalent benefit you had not before discovered. Then you may find yourself richer than you believed yourself to be.

Nothing can be called failure until you accept it as such.

V - Lifestyle Balance

Maintaining Sound Health

MOST EVERYONE OF US would like to get the greatest vigor and fullest use from that body of ours. We can if we make certain that we fully understand two important ideas. They are the oneness of the Creator's masterpiece, the human mind-body, and its oneness with all of nature.

We cannot separate the body and the mind, for they are one. Anything that affects the health and vigor of the mind will affect the body. In turn, anything that affects the health of our body will affect the mind. This point is so essential to our understanding of health that we have termed the individual a human mind-body.

We are not only one in the sense of a mind-body, but we are also part of the environment in which we live. We are born into a world of trees and mountains and moonlit skies, peopled with all forms of living things, and subject to the same natural laws that govern all things, even the grain of wheat.

Nothing about life is static or unchanging. There seems to be a constant wave-like motion to life. It is actually a progression of rhythmical patterns. This is one of the factors in our enjoyment of music.

Consider for a moment one of the earlier lessons in which you learned that the subconscious mind worked best when the mind was at rest, best when we live a rhythm of work and play. The greatest research achievements are produced by the subconscious mind, after it has been loaded with the facts, and the mind is then occupied with other thoughts. That is, the mind is playing. Are you giving your subconscious mind a chance to work by playing?

You know, it's a wonderful thing to have a system whereby you can have this old physical frame in fine condition to do anything you want to do. Anytime you want to do it.

First of all, let's take mental attitude - that comes to the head of the list as you notice, because without a health consciousness, in other words, without thinking and acting and being in terms of health, the chances are that you're not going to be healthy.

There is a way of controlling ailments - mental attitude. First of all, there must be no griping in family or occupational relationships. It just hurts the digestion. Now you will notice that every one of these things is in connection with the conditioning of their mental attitude is something that you can control. If you want to do it, no griping in family or occupational relationships.

Now, the reason I mentioned family relationships and occupational relationship is there where you spend most of your life. You're going to allow those relationships to be based upon the friction and misunderstandings and arguments, why you're not going to have good health and you're not going to happy and you're not going to happen. That must be no hatred, no matter how much this person deserves to be hated, you can't afford to do the hating. You just can't afford it because it's bad for your health. It produces stomach ulcers and worse things than that. It produces negative mental attitudes that repels people, instead of attracting them to you and you can't afford that. It attracts to you reprisals in kind, and it hurts digestion.

If you hate people, they'll hate you. They may not say so, but they will. There must be no gossip or slander. That's a pretty hard one to comply with because there's so much wonderful material the gossip about, and the world seems to fit in.

There's no gossip or slander because they attract reprisals and they also hurt the digestion. And that must mean no fear because it indicates friction in human relationships and also hurts the digestion. And also, if there's any fear in your makeup, it indicates very definitely that there's something in your life that needs to be changed or altered.

There must be no envy because it indicates lack of self reliance. And it also hurts the digestion. Now here are just some of the things - there are six things that I give you in a way of dues that will make you able to maintain the mental attitude that is conducive of a health consciousness. And believe you me, the mind, the way you use your mind has more to do with your health and all other things combined. We talk about germs getting into the blood. All you want do, but believe me, nature has set up a marvelous system of doctoring inside of you. And germ or no germ, if that system is working properly, that resistance that's in your physical body will take care of all those germs. Nature has a way of keeping through body resistance, keeping down the supply. So those germs cannot multiply. And the very minute you become worried or annoyed or fear and break down that body resistance, these germs begin to multiply by the billions and trillions and quadrillions. The first thing you know, you really are sick.

The story of civilization is punctuated with greatness achieved by various individuals in spite of physical bankruptcy, because these individuals possessed smoothly functioning minds. Each of them had a definite major purpose, faith in that purpose and plan, and faith in Infinite Intelligence. They understood clearly where they were going and what their problem was.

Negative thinking is destructive. While hypochondria is one type of negative thinking, it is not the only form that is destructive to the mind-body. If we consider any disease and its symptoms as a spectrum, like that of sunlight when the light is broken into its components –

from the deep reds through the yellows and blues to the deep violets – we can arrange the symptoms and physical effects, the pain, the mental distress that distort the body in a similar long line. Somewhere in the middle of this spectrum of any disease is a small part of the line that really represents the disease. The remainder of the spectrum on both sides of this small area is due to fear, anxiety, negative thinking and maladjustment.

That which the mind expects and demands the mind has a way of producing, and it will bring sickness as readily as it will bring sound health.

This mind-body of ours, to reach great heights of successful living and smooth efficient functioning, must first learn to live a rhythmical life, in harmony with the world of living and non-living things about us, and in harmony with natural laws that govern these rhythms of life.

Budgeting Time and Money

IF YOU EVER HAVE FINANCIAL security in this world, you've got to do two things. You've got to budget your time, the use of your time. And you've got to budget your money, your expenditures on your receipts, so that you have a definite plan to go by.

Broadly speaking, there are two classes of people: the drifters and the non-drifters. A non-drifter is a person who has a definite major purpose, a definite plan to attain that purpose, and is busily engaged in carrying out his plan. The non-drifter thinks his own thoughts and assumes full responsibility for them, whether they are right or wrong.

The drifter does no real thinking, but accepts the thoughts, ideas and opinions of others, and acts upon them as if they were his own.

The world is managed by the non-drifters.

The non-drifter is a leader in his self-chosen occupation. The drifter is a follower.

Drifting is a mental and lifelong choice-habit which becomes permanent. The drifter follows the line of least resistance every chance they get, and repeats their mistakes over and over again.

The non-drifter is focused on blazing new trails, trying new approaches, and learning from his mistakes and failures – as well as those of people around him and by studying histories and biographies of successful people.

The non-drifter acts always to achieve their definite of purpose. They always apply the habit of going the extra mile in all actions. They move on their own personal initiative, regardless of others.

The non-drifter controls all of their habits of thought and action through strict self-discipline, maintains a positive mental attitude, and thinks only of achieving that definite purpose. Persistence supports all of his actions, so applied faith brings his creative vision into form around him.

The non-drifter surrounds himself with a master mind group so that they can share their cooperative knowledge and experience and fulfill their common purpose.

The non-drifter regularly takes personal inventory of themselves to recognize their own weaknesses, so they can refine and build on their native talents

There are nine major areas outlined below that you can use as a measuring stick to take personal self-inventory.

Occupation

DRIFTERS NEVER SELECT an occupation which is suited to their education, or to their mental and spiritual temperaments.

The non-drifter chooses his own occupation with care, and so is engaged in a work which truly is a labor of love. Into this, they willingly project his creative ability, his enthusiasm, his hopes and aims.

Instead of measuring by the amount of hours required, the non-drifter evaluates it by how much useful service he provides – by going the extra mile. The spirit expended while the work is accomplished also counts, for that spirit gives one the pride of achievement.

The non-drifter gets two kinds of pay. One comes in his pay envelope; the other (and far the greater) comes from the skill and experience he acquires by rendering the best possible service, and in the good will he creates through willing cooperation.

Habitual Thought

THE DRIFTER THINKS idly. They daydream and meander through their day. They make no attempt to discipline or control their thoughts, and never learns the difference between positive and negative thinking. Drifting thought is the cause of work accidents in almost all instances.

The non-drifter focuses his own mind through self-discipline, and organizes for executing definite plans. They keep his focus on the ends they desire, and off the things they do not want or need.

A positive mental attitude is the most important riches of life, and it can't be learned by any drifter. You can only achieve it through a scrupulous regard for time, and self-discipline as a habit. A positive mental attitude is the power which makes budgeting your time both effective and productive.

A positive mental attitude can't grow in a weed-filled mind. It requires cultivation, through carefully disciplined habits of thought.

Business, Professional and Personal Relationships

YOUR GREATEST SUCCESS is attained through friendly cooperation, in careful association other non-drifters. Harmony in your various human relationships leads to confidence, which leads to friendly cooperation.

All through history, our culture's greatest tragedies were created by people spending so much time in useless friction, disagreements and misunderstandings with others. Budgeting time could have easily avoided all of these.

It's rare to find two people anywhere, at any time, who are align with one another in perfect harmony and mutual understanding. Take inventory of the relationships of those you know best, and realize how true this is. Friction, conflict and misunderstandings interrupt friendly relationships and cause useless waste of time. While common sense should convince anyone that harmony is the only common meeting ground people can use to coordinate their efforts for mutual benefit.

Successful business and professional men do not waste time quarreling. They pool their time and direct it to definite ends with telling effect. Unsuccessful people are found burning most of their time in interpersonal friction.

Time and human relationships must both be properly organized and utilized achieve your success. Organize your time efficiently, relate to others harmoniously, and you may get anything and everything you want out of life. You only have to establish a definite purpose, work out a plan, and put that plan into action – harmoniously with others.

Habits of Health

THE AVERAGE MAN PAYS more attention to the care of his automobile than he does to the care of his own health. The drifter fills his stomach with whatever his appetite craves. Even though it may be indigestible. Later, when their system is responding with pain, they reach for the nearest drug. At last, their digestive system can't take any more abuse and forces them into a forced slowdown with a cold or a fever.

The drifter knows that any vehicle they drive must have maintenance – not just fuel, but oil, tune-ups, lubrication, and moderate driving instead of high speeds. They don't recognize that their own physical body also requires regular, systematic servicing to maintain good health.

The drifter calls the doctor and then expects the physician to cure in a few days all the damage they have been committing to their body over months or years. At last, after the doctor has helped Nature to restore their health, they just start their habitual self-abuse all over again.

Religion

TO MANY MEN RELIGION is something they accept as a practice on Sundays, but don't apply or live through every moment of their life during the rest of the week. Religion's benefit inspires the individual to recognize that their own spiritual qualities. To utilize those qualities to achieve a better life, their definite purpose. The value of a man's religion lies through deeds, and not mere words.

A person's religion can protect them against their fears. A passive religion, like a passive attitude towards any definite purpose, accomplishes nothing. Like your physical body, you need spiritual food – in a properly balanced diet. Religion is the greatest of all sources from which spiritual food may be obtained.

True religion gives you humility, sympathy for the unfortunate, and enables your willingness to go the extra mile. True religion leads to harmony in your relationships, and enables the Golden Rule. With an applied religion, you are led to enjoying a labor of love, one of the key riches of life.

True religion enables your positive mental attitude and being able to live and let live. This is the source of your creative vision, and inspires the attainment of whatever positions in life you want.

Use of Spare Time

SPARE TIME IS ALL THE time you have left over after work and sleep. You can tell your own future by how you use your spare time. Because this period is where you can direct your extra imagination and creative thoughts toward any end. Spare time where you prepare for greater responsibilities. Where luck is defined as "opportunity met with preparation" – *this* is the time where you can prepare for any eventuality coming your way.

Few, if any, people have attained higher brackets of success without having found themselves in some incident of failure or defeat. The underlying truth is that every adversity carries with it the seed of an equivalent or a greater benefit. And it's your spare time that allows you to review your past failures to extract that benefit.

Self-discipline, will power and your definite purpose are needed to organize your spare time. As you organize and refine your extra time, you may find that more becomes availble.

Un-budgeted Spending

EVERY SUCCESSFUL BUSINESS and industry operates on a strict budget which accounts for both time and money expenses. Every successful individual must budget his own life on such a basis as well.

Wasting time is perhaps worse than wasting money. But look around your life and see if you have accumulated "stuff" that won't help you attain that definite purpose you've chosen.

To many people developing the habit of budgeting their spending won't be easy to adopt or pleasant. Mastering this early will ensure your independence well after your top earning years.

Family Relationships

THE FAMILY RELATIONSHIP is the most important of all human relationships. Its success requires harmony, understanding, sympathy and friendly cooperation from every family member. The parents of the family cannot succeed in their chosen occupation without the peace of mind which grows from their home harmony. Familial harmony results from careful planning, budgeting family income and purchases, and fixing family responsibilities for every family member.

Where a couple work together harmoniously, with a definite and common goal, they can find solutions to all problems, regardless of how serious.

Drifting in important family relationships leads to the divorce courts, poverty, misery and misunderstandings. Every family should be a closed corporation in which every member of the family has responsibilities to discharge his duties for the good of the group, and the corporation should be managed as any well managed business is conducted, with definiteness of purpose, harmony, loyalty and oneness of purpose.

Accurate Thinking

RELYING ON GUESSES and assumptions instead of gathering, organizing and classifying facts is a common drifter habit. Without facts, you can't build plans and reach decisions.

The non-drifter has only opinions built from exactly gathered facts, or reasonable hypotheses based on known facts. They never express an opinion not based on actual facts.

Accurate thinking isn't a present you can receive. It's an art built on a disciplined habit. Refer to the earlier chapter on this subject to refine your own thinking talents.

Maintaining Your Natural Balance

THIS CHAPTER SUMMARIZES an analysis of a law of nature which is the basis of all of our habits, both good and bad.

This law is a vital part of the seventeen success principles. It is the means by which you and every other person can put into operation an irresistible power. One that ensures your aims and purposes are attained almost automatically by the action of your habits.

I have named this law "Natural Balance" because it is the law which gives definiteness of action to everything which moves throughout the entire universe. It keeps the stars and planets in their accustomed places, and it fixes the life patterns of every living thing, from the smallest insects to the largest animal. Only excepting humans, who have been given the means by which they may use this law to establish their own habits and determine their own desires and movements throughout life.

Natural balance binds every living thing other than Man with what we call instinct, but Man can rise above these fixed patterns that lower forms of life use to survive with and establish his *own* patterns. This privilege, as I have mentioned in former chapters, is the only thing over which man has complete power of control and direction.

It is interesting to observe that the Creator never gives Man any form of riches without sending along with it ways Man may do whatever he pleases with those riches.

In order that you may get the full benefit of this chapter on natural balance, it will be necessary to review the earlier sixteen principles of success I have already described – particularly the first principle: definiteness of purpose.

LIKE EVERY OTHER NATURAL law, natural balance has both a positive and a negative potential application.

The negative application of this law is called hypnotic rhythm. That means, among other possible results, it fastens upon individuals who neglect to fix their thoughts upon what they most desire in life. Here, the law automatically acts to fix our minds on the things we *don't* desire and attracts to us the physical counterpart of those.

Understand this principle of the law of natural balance, and you will have a better conception as to how essential it is to keep your mind occupied with your life pattern – the one you've created with the things and circumstances you desire – until this new pattern is taken over and made permanent by natural balance.

Natural balance is the watchdog that looks over your shoulder all through life. It examines every thought you release, every act you engage in, and forces on you the penalties or the rewards you've earned by your actions.

When you understand the principle of natural balance, it is clear enough that you can either go through your life without using the power of this law to achieve the circumstances and the desires you voluntarily chose – or, by your own neglect, allow the same law to force you to pay the penalties above.

You have the power of choice here, the same as in all other things, but your neglect to exercise this power brings certain, if not always swift, retribution upon you. Perhaps you now see why I warned you above that the two sealed envelopes were not imaginary, but real. And of course you now understand that you must avail yourself of the benefits of one or be forced to accept the penalties of the other. There is no halfway compromise for any human being.

Consider this profound truth, and you will probably get a more impressive understanding of the power that is available to you through the application of the full 17 success principles of the Science of Success.

This can give you a better understanding why these 17 principles have spread throughout the world without organized business management behind them. And why this Science of Success philosophy is believed to have brought personal success to more people than has any other. Especially those philosophies designed to help individuals to take possession of their own minds.

The nearest to a description of the law of natural balance I have seen is Emerson's law of Compensation. Here he clearly established the truth that nothing ever just happens by luck, but every effect has its definite cause. We often observe effects from the causes of which we cannot isolate or understand. If you will read Emerson's essay on Compensation again in view of what I have said about the law of natural balance, you may get much more from it than you absorbed from it previously.

———————

HERE'S SOME ILLUSTRATIONS as to how the law of natural balance operates:

One, first of all, let me call your attention to the fact that natural balance fixes the habits of the electrons and protons of matter so that their relationship and chemical behavior always follow the same pattern. And so we see that everything throughout the universe comes under the influence of natural balance and everything moves and exists by a pattern which is immutable and enduring – except the human species, who, as I have said, can break the habits established by natural balance which affect them. We can set up in their place habits of our own choice.

Two, natural balance fixes the pattern of every form of vegetation which grows from the soil of the Earth so that each thing reproduces after its own pattern. A grain of wheat always reproduces other grains of wheat but never makes the mistake of producing oats or some other form of growth. An oak tree always springs from an acorn but never from any other cause, the pattern having been permanently fixed in the acorn by the law of natural balance. One atom of hydrogen and two atoms of oxygen combined always produce water, never anything else, because the pattern of their chemical reaction has been fixed by natural balance.

Three, when the human mind is focused on a definite major purpose, the law of natural balance goes into action immediately and attracts to the individual the material equivalent of that purpose, and the procedure is inexorable and never varies. However, hypnotic rhythm, the negative application of the law, will just as definitely attract to one all the undesirable things and circumstances which the mind is allowed to dwell upon, such as poverty, ill health, failure, fear, and all other undesirable things.

Four, natural balance expressing itself through the emotion of sex is the means by which every living thing perpetuates its species. Understand this truth, and you will better understand the irresistible forces of the profound emotion of sex, the means by which nature creates all living things. You will also better understand why it is so essential to learn how to transmute the emotion of sex into the carrying out of your aims and purposes.

Five, we sometimes hear people speak of successful men as being "on the beam", by which they mean that those who enjoy success have established a success thought pattern in their minds which natural balance has picked up and carried out to its logical conclusion.

You are on the beam when you take possession of your mind, direct it to definite ends, with a spirit of belief in your attainment of those ends, and keep your mind busy in carrying out your purpose instead of allowing it to drift to subjects you wish to avoid.

You are on the beam when you can truthfully say, "I know precisely what I want from life, and I have faith I will get it." You are not on the beam when you have no definite major purpose and you are drifting aimlessly through life.

People who are failures also are on the beam, but they are on the negative side of that beam because they have neglected to use those riches which came over with them at birth, and they have placed themselves under the influence of hypnotic rhythm, which is the negative application of natural balance.

———

THERE IS ONE WORD WHICH doctors dread, and it is the word "fixation," which means that a sick person believes in his sickness as something which cannot be cured.

But fixations can become a priceless asset by those who have learned how to develop fixations in their minds based on the things they desire most in life.

Natural balance is the power which makes fixations permanent.

You should have a definite fixation based on your major purpose in life, but you are the only one who can create this fixation. You can do it by taking possession of your own mind and keeping it directed toward the attainment of your major purpose. If you will do this by following all the instructions I have given you in these chapters, in a short time you will find yourself on the beam and headed directly toward everything you desire and deserve to receive.

Finally, remember that your mental attitude is something you control outright. You must use self-discipline until you create a thought pattern or thought habits which keep your mental attitude positive at all times. Your mental attitude is important because it acts as a magnet which attracts to you everything, every circumstance which makes you what you are and where you are.

If you wish to keep on the beam that leads to success, be sure that you give natural balance a thought pattern based on the things you want most in life – and it will do the rest.

SCIENCE OF SUCCESS COURSE LESSONS

———

THE FULL 17 LESSONS in the PMA Science of Success Course are available from this publisher:

Lesson One - Definiteness of Purpose

Lesson Two - The Master Mind

Lesson Three - Applied Faith

Lesson Four - Going the Extra Mile

Lesson Five - Pleasing Personality

Lesson Six - Personal Initiative

Lesson Seven - Positive Mental Attitude

Lesson Eight - Enthusiasm

Lesson Nine - Self-Discipline

Lesson Ten - Accurate Thinking

Lesson Eleven - Focused Attention

Lesson Twelve - Teamwork

Lesson Thirteen - Learning from Adversity and Defeat

Lesson Fourteen - Creative Vision

Lesson Fifteen - Maintaining Sound Health

Lesson Sixteen - Budgeting Time and Money

Lesson Seventeen - Natural Balance (Cosmic Habitforce)

———————————

THESE LESSONS ARE EACH being made available in all possible formats, including an online self-study version. Additional related courses are under development as well.

Visit https://livesensical.com/go/pma-sos/ for our latest updates and expansions (as well as special offers and discounts...)

GOAL ACHIEVEMENT COURSES AVAILABLE

———

BELOW ARE A PARTIAL list of the ever-expanding courses currently available on our site as this book is published.

Many are no-cost to sign up, and the rest are worth far more than you could ever pay. Because once you master the subject of goal achievement, you can literally get everything you want out of life.

You'll recognize many of these. These courses have been created and produced from the material of several classics. So you know the data is tested and can be trusted.

════════════

THE "STRANGEST SECRET" Course

Earl Nightingale's Gold Record is available for your study, in audio and video format, along with downloadable handouts.

If You Can Count to Four Course

Dr. J. B. Jones borrowed $10,000 from friends and built a 10-figure national business within five years – starting from his living room. Here's how he did it – and how you can, too. Just four simple steps...

How to Completely Change Your Life in 30 Seconds

Based on some of Earl Nightingale's most memorable recordings, this course covers several areas of goal achievement, entrepreneurship, and many related subjects. Derived from the bestselling book of that title.

Napoleon Hill's PMA: Science of Success Course

Newly recovered from archived material, this master course was the final and updated version of Hill's Individual Achievement Philosophy that you're familiar with from his "Think and Grow Rich". The 10 hours of original lectures and his out-of-print teaching guide have been distilled into 17 modules of audio and video lessons. A lifetime of riches that updates his books into readily-absorbed formats.

Visit https://calm.li/CurrentCourses *now* **to get started.**

YOUR WORLD IS FILLED WITH STRANGE SECRETS

...that are hidden in plain sight.

THEY ARE STRANGE BECAUSE they are commonly known in our literature and history.

Solutions to poverty, lack, disappointment.

And people who discover them think they are the first to figure them out.

There are tons of books out there that essentially say the same thing.
And have existed through all our long written history and literature.

This is what Earl Nightingale found when he wrote and recorded his 78RPM LP record in *1957*. And it was such a breakthrough that it became the first Gold record of its kind - *all without any advertising.*

*Because he struck a common chord that explains **all** success.*

It's time for you to get everything you want out of life.

Let me give you a small book that tells you exactly how this works.

To help you, I've taken Nightingale's original recording and made its transcript available for you, along with short versions of the books he recommends on that recording. Plus some other related essays and articles. All slim enough to fit on your smartphone for ready review - anywhere, any time.

All at no-charge, no cost.

It doesn't cost you even a penny to kickstart your success.

To get what you want. Everything you want.

Limited Time Offer

You can download your own copy of this book – as long as still available.

Visit: [1]https://calm.li/SSC-NF

BOOKS BY RELATED AUTHORS

By Earl Nightingale:

How to Completely Change Your Life in 30 Seconds[1]

Why Ninety-Five Fail, Only Five Succeed[2]

How to Prevent Stress From Ruining Your Life[3]

How to Mine Your Own Acres of Diamonds[4]

How Creative People Win[5]

2 Amazing Ways to Solve Your Problems[6]

7 Strange Secrets to Winning Big[7]

The $25,000 Idea[8]

Earl Nightingale's Strangest Secret Library[9]

----

1. https://livesensical.com/book/completely-change-your-life-30-seconds/

2. https://livesensical.com/book/ninety-five-fail-five-succeed-earl-nightingale/

3. https://livesensical.com/book/prevent-stress-ruining-life/

4. https://livesensical.com/book/entrepreneurship-mine-acres-diamonds/

5. https://livesensical.com/book/creative-people-win-earl-nightingale/

6. https://livesensical.com/book/creative-people-win-earl-nightingale/

7. https://livesensical.com/book/7-strange-secrets-winning-big-get-happy-money-health/

8. https://livesensical.com/book/25000-idea-simple-ways-effective-goal-achievement/

9. https://livesensical.com/book/earl-nightingales-strangest-secret-library/

BY NAPOLEON HILL:

The Updated and Complete Think and Grow Rich[10]

The Master Key to Riches[11]

The Magic Ladder to Success[12]

10 Easy Lessons in Cosmic Habitforce[13]

The Law of Success[14]

—————————

BY J. B. JONES:

If You Can Count to Four...[15]

How to Get Everything You Want Out of Life[16]

—————————

BY CLAUDE M. BRISTOL:

Magic of Believing – the Science of Goal Achievement[17]

The Magic of Believing Collection[18]

---

10. https://livesensical.com/book/think-grow-rich-updated-complete/

11. https://livesensical.com/book/master-key-riches-sequel-think-grow-rich/

12. https://livesensical.com/book/magic-ladder-success-prequel-think-grow-rich/

13. https://livesensical.com/book/10-easy-lessons-cosmic-habitforce/

14. https://livesensical.com/book/law-success-law-attraction/

15. https://livesensical.com/book/
    if-you-can-count-to-four-by-james-breckenridge-jones-self-improvement-books/

16. https://livesensical.com/book/get-everything-want-life/

17. https://livesensical.com/book/magic-believing-science-goal-achievement/

18. https://calm.li/MOB-Coll

—————

BY DOROTHEA BRANDE:

Wake Up and Live![19]

—————

BY WALLACE D. WATTLES:

Science of Getting Rich[20]

—————

BY DR. ROBERT C. WORSTELL:

Freedom Is - period[21]

Winning Your Infinite Freedom[22]

Make Yourself Great Again![23]

The Art of Wonk[24]

—————

OR VISIT OUR ONLINE bookstore at:

https://calm.li/LivingSensical

19. https://livesensical.com/book/wake-live-dorothea-brande/

20. https://livesensical.com/book/science-getting-rich/

21. https://livesensical.com/book/freedom-period-dr-robert-c-worstell/

22. https://livesensical.com/book/winning-infinite-freedom-complete-series-2006-2011/

23. https://livesensical.com/book/make-great-complete-collection-mindset-stacking/

24. https://livesensical.com/book/art-wonk-compleat/

MORE BOOKS YOU MAY LIKE

ALL OUR LATEST RELEASES[1]

Both fiction and non-fiction – each with links to major online book outlets as well as author discounts.

The Strangest Secret Library[2]

All the full references mentioned in Earl Nightingale's Strangest Secret Library available for instant download – through your online book outlet of choice or with our publisher's discount.

Books on Success and Goal Achievement[3]

Our collection of modern and classic references on how you can become a personal success and achieve your own goals – to get *everything* you want out of life.

Books on Writing & [4]Publishing[5]

Our collection of modern and classic references on how to improve your writing in our modern self-publishing age.

Speculative F[6]iction [7]Modern Parables[8]

1. https://livesensical.com/books/?utm_campaign=related-book-ad&utm_source=ebook

2. https://livesensical.com/book-series/
   strangest-secret-library/?utm_campaign=related-book-ad&utm_source=ebook

3. https://livesensical.com/book-series/how-to-completely-change-your-life/

4. https://livesensical.com/book-series/
   publishing-and-writing/?utm_campaign=related-book-ad&utm_source=ebook

5. https://livesensical.com/book-series/
   publishing-and-writing/?utm_campaign=related-book-ad&utm_source=ebook

Our short stories and anthologies – all in order of most recent release.

Classic Fiction[9]

Our ever-expanding collection of fiction stories that are hard to find, yet their stories never grow old. Perfect entertainment when the too-modern world becomes stale...

---

6. https://livesensical.com/book-series/

   fiction/?utm_campaign=related-book-ad&utm_source=ebook

7. https://livesensical.com/book-series/

   fiction/?utm_campaign=related-book-ad&utm_source=ebook

8. https://livesensical.com/book-series/

   fiction/?utm_campaign=related-book-ad&utm_source=ebook

9. https://livesensical.com/book-series/fiction-classics/

DID YOU LIKE THIS BOOK?

———

HOW ABOUT LEAVING A review with the vendor?

Otherwise (or in addition) you can leave your recommendations on:

- **Bookbub**[1]

The whole point is to enable others to find books that you liked reading.

Which then helps you find more great books to read.

And...

Feel free to share this book!

1. https://www.bookbub.com/recommendations

Did you love *Napoleon Hill's PMA: Science of Success Course - An Introduction*? Then you should read *Make Yourself Great Again - Complete Collection*[2] by Dr. Robert C. Worstell!

You're Already Wired for Exceptional Success

BUT: Those same programs also have given you your greatest failures.

If you've ever had a complete melt-down, a real failure of your mindset, where the world has seemingly gone to hell and stayed there, you're not alone.

it's just sad to tell you that it's your own damned fault.

What makes it worse is to find out that all you need to succeed was already programmed into you – and has been since you were born.

Then how did you get into that mess?

---

2. https://books2read.com/u/mV7kQA

3. https://books2read.com/u/mV7kQA

By believing what people told you- as you were raised,- and in every school you went to,- all your on the job training,- every movie you ever saw,- or song you ever heard.

All those lessons and examples just helped you believe in something other than your own ability to become great.

Most of what we are told these days are that the environment makes the individual. However, this has only really been taught since just after World War II. Long, long before that, there were many schools of thought which held that the individual creates their own success in this world, or lack of it.

And that is a far longer tradition, across our 10,000 years of culture, back through our verbal traditions and storytellers.

Some of our oldest traditions, such as the Tibetan Book of the Dead, say that as children we have complete access to all the world's knowledge – up to the point we learn to talk. And other traditions say that we can each still tap into unlimited knowledge. Some studies begun in the 1950's and verified through testing, have shown this to still be true.

Unfortunately, this isn't what Conventional Wisdom says. Most Science disagrees. And it isn't what any government or school wants you to believe. All the best authorities...

However, one of the oldest phrases, published in books in various formats throughout all of our recorded works, says the same thing in various ways:

We Become What We Think About.

What you think and how you think is up to you. How you think consistently, the mental habits you've developed, are those you chose for yourself.

If you build those mental habits stacked on top of unproved, untested data, then you risk your sanity because you listened to all these sources and chose to think that way.

The economic crash of 2008 affected a lot of people adversely. But a lot more people survived.

The U.S. election of 2016 affected a lot of people adversely. But a lot more people survived.

There will always be more adverse situations ahead. Because that's the cyclical history of this mudball we live on.

But you don't have to repeat these failures, these crashes.

And now, this story is complete.

This series of 4 books now answers all the questions and takes you right back to the beginning to learn even more. Because this subject is as deep as you want to take it. You are referenced to current newsmakers as examples as well as principles back before our 10,000 years of history started.

This is a landmark volume you'll want as a reference, along with its sister handbook, The Strangest Secret Library. And your life is guaranteed to never be the same...

Get Your Copy Now.

Read more at https://livesensical.com/book-author/ dr-robert-c-worstell/.

Also by Dr. Robert C. Worstell

Make Yourself Great Again Library
Why You Got All That Stuff
The Art of Wonk, Compleat

Masters of Copywriting
Breakthrough Copywriter 2.0: An Advertising Field Guide to Eugene
M. Schwartz' Classic

Mindset Stacking Guides
Make Yourself Great Again Part 1
Make Yourself Great Again Part 2
Make Yourself Great Again Part 3
Make Yourself Great Again Part 4
Choose. Believe. Win.
Make Yourself Great Again - Complete Collection
Go Thunk Yourself, Again!

PMA Science of Success

Napoleon Hill's PMA: Science of Success Course - An Introduction

Really Simple Writing & Publishing
How To Write And Publish For Free
Backwards Book Publishing: Save Time, Earn More, Work Less
Writing-Publishing Survival Guide
Author Freedom Guidebook
How to Stop Feeding the Beast
A Completely Unauthorized Instafreebie Guidebook
How I Survived My First Year of Fiction Writing
How to Become an Instant Author in 30 Seconds
Becoming a Wealthy Writer
Marketers & Writers - Scammers & Dupes

Standalone
Farm Less, Profit More: Lessons in Regenerative Grazing

Watch for more at https://livesensical.com/book-author/
dr-robert-c-worstell/.

Midwest Journal Press
Finding You Books that Continue to Change Your Life

About the Publisher

"Finding you books that continue to change your life."

A veteran publishing imprint and a practical philosophy for life, Midwest Journal Press has been active publishing new and established authors since 2006.

We take advantage of the new Print on Demand and ebook technologies to enable wider discovery for authors.

We publish in most of the major genres of fiction and non-fiction.

Our current emphasis is in speculative fiction modern parables.

For More Information, Visit:

https://livesensical.com/midwestjournalpress/